Feng Shui Simplified

A Family Guide to Creating Harmony and Love in Your Home

Nancy Stohn

Ordering information can be found on the Internet at her website www.interiorswithfengshui.com

Note for Librarians: a cataloguing record for this book that includes the Dewey Classification and US Library of Congress numbers is available from the National Library of Canada. The complete cataloguing record can be obtained from the National Library's online database at: www.nlc-bnc.ca/amicus/index-e.html
ISBN 1-4120-4342-5

Editors: Dr. Carol Mazuy, Catherine Jaspersohn, Larissa Hordynsky

Photography: Nancy Stohn, Dr. Carol Mazuy

Cover Design and Artworks: Cheryl Schainfeld

Cover Image: Stephen Simpson/Getty Images

Layout, Illustrations, and Back Cover Design and Photography: Catherine Jaspersohn

---

TRAFFORD on-demand publishing service™

Suite 6E, 2333 Government St., Victoria, BC, Canada V8T 4P4
Phone 250-383-6864 Toll-free 1-888-232-4444 (Canada & US)
Fax 250-383-6804 E-mail info@trafford.com
Website www.trafford.com
Trafford catalogue # 04-2150 www.trafford.com/robots/04-2150.html

10 9 8 7 6 5 4 3

DEDICATION

I dedicate this book to my granddaughters Courtney and Sydney. They have guided me with love and inspiration to write a book for the benefit of other children and their families.

Along with me, they want the children of the world to have a life filled with love, learning, good health, and the ability to play.

ACKNOWLEDGEMENTS

In the design of a room, classroom, or office, the energy must flow freely like a river for the people to receive the benefits of love, learning, health, and the ability to play. I want you to receive the gifts of living a fulfilled life with Feng Shui.

My book has been made possible because I had the love and support and participation from my family and friends. My special thanks to the following people:

Dr. Carol Mazuy, Cheryl Schainfeld, Catherine Jaspersohn, Angel Thompson, Larissa Hordynsky, Beth Cuzzone, Barbara Marcus, Bruce Richardson, Judy Carp, Jane Cohen, Paula Bernstein, Jack Albertson, Susan Ruder, Ruthann Saphier, KaRecia Lodge, Sam Green, Mike Heller, and my fellow directors of the Global Abundance Alliance as well as my Landmark Power and Contribution course friends.

Proceeds from the sale of this book will be used to fund UNICEF and other programs for children.

About the Author

Nancy Stohn is an interior designer, space planner, and art consultant. She has an interior design and Feng Shui consulting business, and provides seminars on Feng Shui for architects, interior designers, and college students.

For more than 30 years, Nancy has designed interior spaces for businesses and residences in New York, Texas, and Boston. Nancy has a BA in Art History. She graduated from the New York School of Interior Design and has a certificate from the Compass School of Feng Shui at Southeast University in Nanking, China. She has also studied the Buddhist Black Sect School of Feng Shui, the Forms School, and the Pyramid School, with Angel Thompson and the Feng Shui Institute of America.

An Allied Member of the American Society of Interior Design, Nancy is currently on the faculty of the Boston Architectural Center and Brookline Center for Adult Education and provides seminars for the architectural and design communities as well as is a Feng Shui Consultant. Nancy is also on the Board of Directors of the Fuller Craft Museum in Brockton, Massachusetts. For more about the author, visit her website at www.interiorswithfengshui.com

Table of Contents

Feng Shui Simplified

A Family Guide to Creating Harmony and Love in Your Home

What is Feng Shui?

Feng Shui (pronounced *fung schway*) is the ancient Chinese art of placement based on respect for order, harmony, and the balance of nature. The words mean "wind" and "water," respectively. Feng Shui principles are based on centuries old Chinese beliefs that combine knowledge of the mystical forces of the universe with a practical approach to planning. I will show you how to apply these principles to create a balance, both physical and emotional, in your home and for your family.

Feng Shui originated thousands of years ago in China. The emperors and ruling political forces needed to know when and where to plant crops, information vital to the successful harvests that would replenish the treasury and ensure the good health and prosperity of the dynasty. Feng Shui was a closely guarded discipline, and those who kept its secrets were highly respected scientists, architects, astronomers, and land surveyors. As practiced today, Feng Shui includes a blend of common sense, logic, reason, and astrological calculations. When you use these principles to connect the design of the rooms in your home with the environmental, lifestyle, and psychological needs of your family, you will create spaces that are supportive, nurturing, and deeply satisfying. Everyone who lives in these spaces can flourish.

A great many books have been written about Feng Shui as this art form continues to gain popularity. Some cover the spiritual aspects of Feng Shui, its history, and its complexities in detail; others take a more simplistic approach. My intention in writing this book is to give parents a simple and straightforward approach to changing the dynamics of the energy in their home. Using the principles of Feng Shui, you will ultimately create a healthy and harmonious environment for yourselves and your children. I will not attempt to reinvent the wheel or reiterate the detailed background of this very rich subject matter. For a thorough review of the art of Feng Shui and its origins, please see the bibliography.

The Four Schools of Feng Shui

Feng Shui has undergone many changes over 4,000 years. The basic principles have developed in different ways, into what are now four distinct schools. They can be a source of confusion and, at times, appear contradictory.

The oldest is the **Form School**, which uses the surrounding landscape, topography, water formations, and the Feng Shui animals (tiger, dragon, tortoise, snake, and phoenix) to orient the house or business. Observations would tell us from which direction the prevailing winds were coming and our homes would be built in protective sites.

The **Compass School** emerged and dominated as urbanization destroyed the natural forms. The Compass School uses the *luopan* (pronounced *loopan*) or compass, giving us the directions that determine how the energy in each part of the building influences its occupants' energy in all directions, based on the landform or heavenly body to be found there. Interpreting these energies suggest suitable sites. The effects of the earth, sun, and planets are all important in the Compass School.

The **Buddhist Black Sect School** relies on Buddhism in intention and contributed to traditional Feng Shui by including religious, spiritual, and magical practices, as well as prayers and chants to break bad spells, bless surroundings, chase away building ghosts, and purify the environment. This sect has been very sympathetic to the Western need to interpret traditional Chinese concepts through contemporary thought and practice.

The **Pyramid School** is the most recent interpretation. It speaks to the issue of the human experience of place. It aims to cast more light on the mysteries of how the physical world impacts the human experience. Therefore it is more intuitive. The cures recommended should be tailored to the individual. We must be comfortable with whatever changes are made using our personal preference and custom. For example, if I choose not to use wind chimes, I can try using a flag or a windsock. Adjustments based on our personal beliefs result in less rigidity.

A well-designed and accessorized living room provides a calming environment for the family.

In ***Feng Shui Simplified***, I have used a combination of the Compass and Pyramid Schools. The inclusion of both allows us to accomplish the changes we have to make for the harmony and balance to occur in our environments.

Part I: What Can Feng Shui Do for Your Family?

Ancient Beginnings Relating to Placement

Feng Shui is called the art of placement because it explores the connection between person and place. At its core is the knowledge that the space around us affects our well-being. In fact, we usually refer to Feng Shui as the "feel" of a place. Our goal, when applying the principles of Feng Shui, is to achieve alignment and balance through proper arrangement of objects within and around our homes. I will stress this repeatedly.

Practitioners use Feng Shui to transform a home or other building, like an office space or a hotel, or a school classroom, into an environmental opportunity for happiness. Our home is the place we have chosen to live in. We have filled its interior spaces with material possessions, some currently in use and other possessions begging to be removed. Feng Shui helps us sort through these belongings to create a balanced environment that enhances our happiness and simplifies our lives. It helps our families to thrive and be well.

Applying Feng Shui Principles to Daily Life

The quasi-scientific technique of Feng Shui analyzes the environment and interprets natural earth forms using a mix of geomancy and architectural fortune telling. Although it is mystical and creative, Feng Shui is definitely practical and it works for the believers. The goal is to harmonize and balance the family's personal and natural environments. While the texts are ancient, the classroom is the current world of nature and the space you're in here and now. Because Feng Shui is based on universal truths, it can be experienced by everyone. It is open, reliable, available, and applicable to all family members. Aesthetics, energy flow, and common sense are the basis for the advice offered by Feng Shui practitioners.

Our entire family and we tend to lead hectic lives, dashing between work, home, and carpool, bolting down our meals, and cramming our daily agenda with appointments and "shoulds." Applying the principles of Feng Shui helps prompt a reevaluation that can transform an unsatisfactory existence into a far more fulfilling life. Make the changes I recommend and watch what happens to your family dynamics as the rooms in your house come into balance.

You can easily improve your quality of life by paying attention to the subtle influences in your family environment. That cracked mirror, burnt-out light bulb, broken furniture leg, torn and soiled carpet, broken window, dripping faucet—all are non-aligned, all reflect a problem in a family member's life. Fixing or replacing them will improve your quality of life.

Certain actions and objects raise the whole family's energy level. Flowers make a sick daughter feel better; something new and red in the living room energizes by providing a touch of color. Creating an appealing auditory environment is as important as your visual one: background music can improve the balance of energy. Add a flowering plant to the area where you dine and notice how you feel.

Maybe family members who can already tell whether a space feels good or bad will recognize Feng Shui as something familiar. They will gain a language to describe their intuitions. Now they can consciously embrace nature and the enhanced quality of life that it affords.

Modern life is great with all its material conveniences and toys. But we also have to acknowledge and respect the natural laws that bring our families and us into balance and harmony. This book focuses on helping you to do just that. Its goal is to spark your continued pursuit of family balance and harmony.

What is Chi?

Feng Shui is based on the principle of a subtle electromagnetic life force called *chi* energy. Throughout Asia the belief exists that, in addition to the forces of nature we can see, feel, hear, taste, and smell, there is another force that we are aware of through a sixth sense. Carried by wind, water, light, sound, and the sun's energy, it flows around and through the universe, affecting all aspects of our lives. The motions of T'ai Chi encourage chi to move through the body.

Chi also flows within our body, carrying our thoughts, ideas, and emotions and influencing every cell. When we feel happy, balanced, and positive, our chi is vital and healthy. But when we are feeling emotionally drained, sad, or angry, a negative energy feeds our body's cells and disease can enter our lives. The kind of thoughts we have subtly influence our cellular wellbeing, which may explain why some people manage to improve their health by changing the way they think.

Chi is not elusive; it is how our senses take in experiences from our surroundings. Chi flows through everything, beginning with the energy in our bodies that underlies the practice of acupuncture. An acupuncturist uses needles to unlock the energy channels and enables chi to flow unencumbered through the body. If the energy in our body is flowing freely and easily, we will stay fit and healthy. If however, that energy becomes stagnant, blocked, or erratic, we will feel ill.

The chi energy field extends outside your body and is influenced by your environment. Exercise, food, the clothing that you wear, the weather, the people that you interact with, in fact everything in your environment, affect your chi. You can achieve goals more easily and successfully when you place yourself in a favorable position for your own chi. How your room is designed, decorated, and accessorized can affect the flow of chi. It is therefore vitally important to create a balanced environment through the proper arrangement of objects.

When your environment is clean and clutter free, the chi flows freely, improving your family's well being. High and low ceilings, wide and narrow doors, small double-hung windows and sliding doors all affect chi, increasing or diminishing energy flow. Some architectural components of your home cannot be changed. However, when your home is improperly furnished, under lit, or cluttered, you can make changes. Different areas of the house and different parts of each room attract specific energies, and room layouts and furniture positions can help or hinder the free flow of energy. If the energy is blocked or flows too quickly, problems show up in your life. Clutter stops the energy from circulating and makes it stagnant. Sharp corners are often too harsh and cause the chi currents to bounce off and not go through the area evenly. By making small shifts in placements in your home, you can affect everything that takes place within, from your finances to your relationships to your health and career. People use Feng Shui because it works.

Your own chi mixes and changes with the chi energy around you. An infinite energy field from the universe constantly affects you—the weather, the presence or absence of sunshine, the position of the sun, the phases of the moon, and the seasons. Our behavior and emotions are all related to the movement of the earth and the position of the planets.

Five Types of Chi Energy

There are five different types of chi energy, determined by the five elements of wood, fire, earth, metal, and water:

木 1. **Wood**: Symbolizes Spring, growth, and plant life. In its yin form, it is supple and pliable like the willow; in its yang form as sturdy as an oak. Viewed as a tree, Wood energy is expansive, nurturing, and versatile.

火 2. **Fire**: Symbolizes Summer, fire, and heat. It can bring light, warmth, and happiness or it can erupt, explode, and destroy with great violence. Positively, it stands for honor and fairness; negatively, it stands for aggression and war.

土 3. **Earth:** Symbolizes the nurturing environment that enables seeds to grow in soil, which all living things emanate from and return to. It nurtures, supports, and interacts with each of the other elements. Positively, it denotes fairness, wisdom, and instinct. Negatively, it can smother or represent the nervous anticipation of non-existing problems.

金 4. **Metal:** Symbolizes Autumn and strength. Its nature represents solidity and the ability to contain objects. It is also a conductor. Positively, it represents communication, brilliant ideas, and justice. Negatively, it can suggest destruction, danger, and sadness. It can be beautiful and a precious commodity, or the blade of a weapon.

水 5. **Water:** Symbolizes Winter and water itself, gentle rain, or a storm. It suggests the inner self, art, and beauty. It touches everything. Positively, it nurtures and supports with understanding. Negatively, it can wear down and exhaust. It can suggest fear, nervousness, and stress.

Ideally, each of the elements is represented throughout the rooms in your home, and there is a balance of all the elements.

Characteristics of The Five Elements

	WOOD	FIRE	EARTH	METAL	WATER
Movement of chi	Upwards	Outwards	Downwards	Inwards	Flowing
Direction	East	South	Center & Southwest	West	North
Color	Green	Red & Purple	Yellow & Brown	White, Pink, & Grey	Black
Shape	Tall & rectangular	Serrated, spikes, & triangular	Low, flat, & rectangular	Round, arched, & oval	Irregular, wavy, & curved
Material	Wood, paper, bamboo	Plastic (but kept to a minimum in Feng Shui)	Clay, ceramic, cotton, wool, soft stone, bricks	Metals, hard stone	Glass
Powerful features	Tall plants	Lights, candles, fireplaces	Charcoal in clay containers	Metal objects & mechanical clocks	Water features

Figure 1: Characteristics of each of the five elements.

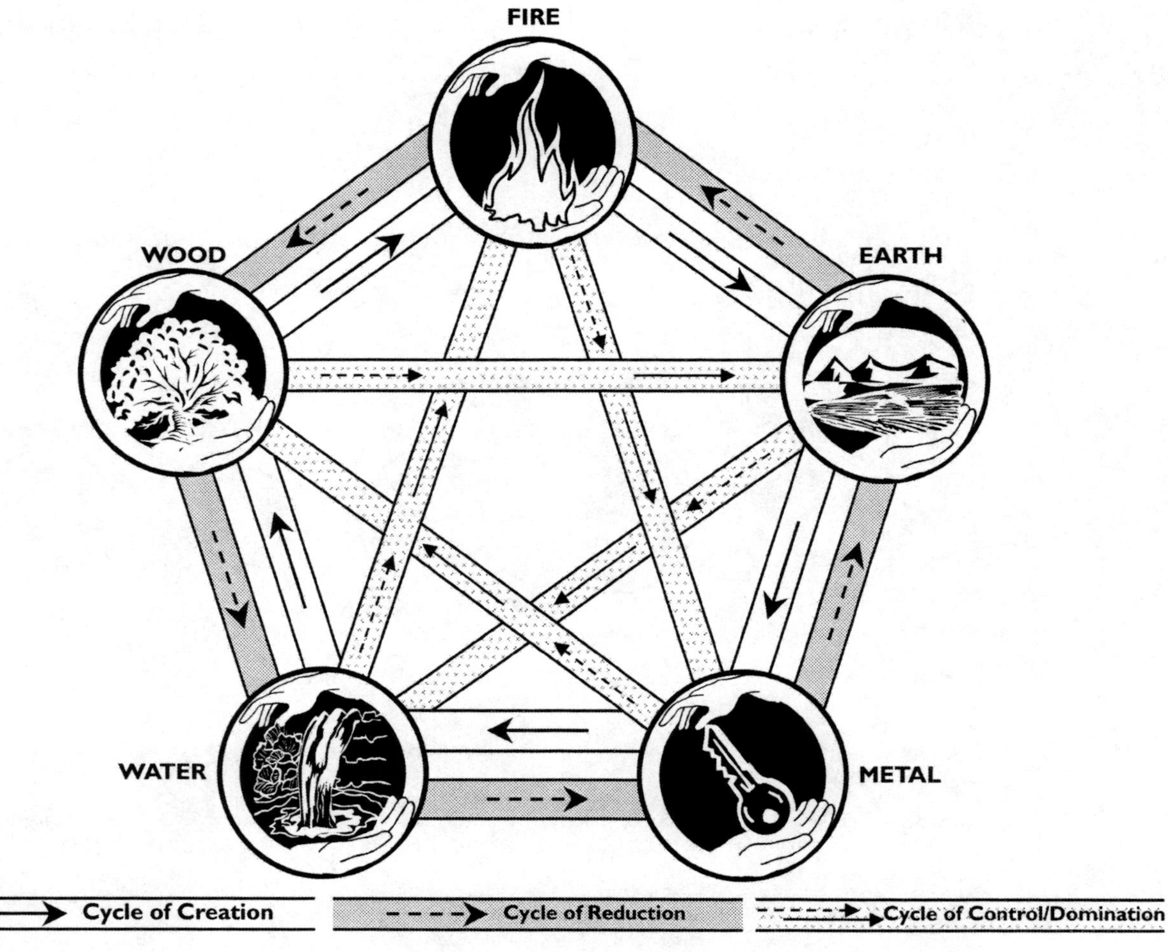

Figure 2: Notice the five elements in relationship with the atmosphere, and how they relate and transform one another. Courtesy of Angel Thompson.

*The **Cycle of Creation** describes Wood creating or sustaining Fire, which generates ash (Earth), which forms ore (Metal), which produces Water through condensation, which feeds and nourishes Wood in a never-ending cycle.*

*The **Cycle of Reduction** describes Fire burning Wood, which absorbs Water, which dissolves Metal, which condenses Earth, which smothers Fire in a never-ending cycle.*

*The **Cycle of Control/Domination** describes Wood consuming Earth, which stops Water, which puts out Fire, which melts Metal, which, when shaped into an ax or saw, chops down Wood.*

What is the Bagua?

According to Feng Shui, properly mapping out and enhancing the Bagua of a home or workplace significantly strengthens the good fortune of its inhabitants. The *Bagua* is an energy map. Once you understand its symbolism, you will be able to use the Bagua to perfect the flow of chi energy in your home, enhance the wellbeing of your family, and improve the parenting of your children. The nine essential principles of courage, stillness, joy, receptivity, synchronicity, integrity, strength, gratitude and connection are integral to who we are and provide a foundation for all members of the family to flourish.

The following is a simplified version of the Bagua:

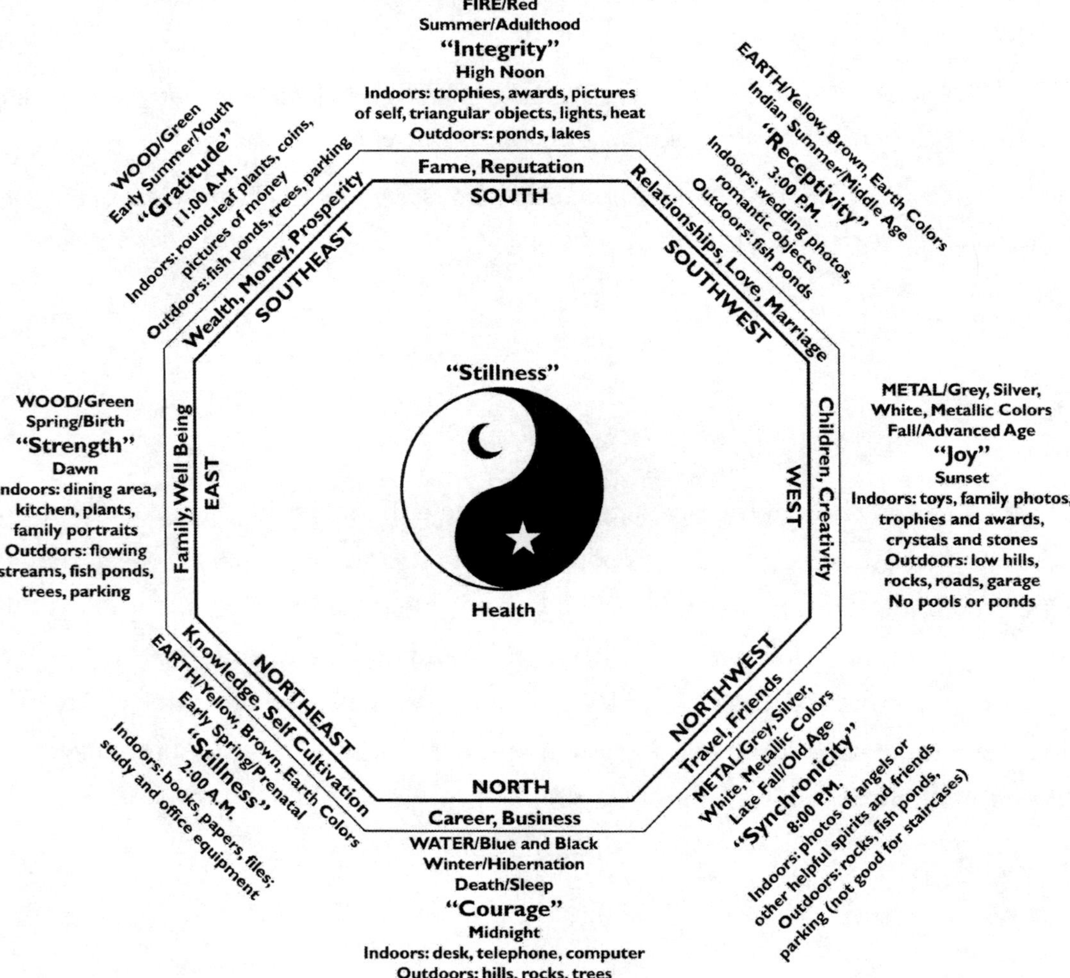

Figure 3: The Bagua Map, showing the energies associated with each of the eight directions. Courtesy of Angel Thompson.

Mapping Out Your Home with the Bagua Map

To begin, draw a plan of the room in your house that you want to analyze first. I would like you to focus on the master bedroom first because the heads of the household exert so much energy on the other family members.

Use a standard compass to determine what direction you are facing when you look straight out the entrance door to the master bedroom. Next, draw a Bagua using the same scale as your room plan. The Bagua does not have to have all its sides equal in length. Only the parallel line pairs of east/west and north/south must be of the same length, i.e., the Bagua can be stretched or shrunk to almost any size:

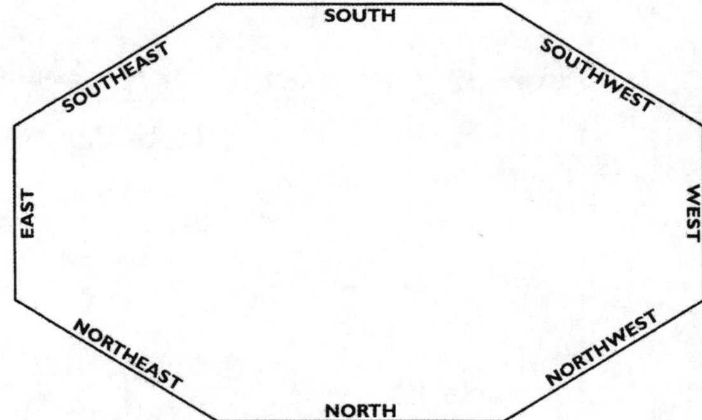

Place the Bagua over the room plan so it fits as much as possible inside the room, matching the directions and aligning the Bagua with the wall holding the entrance door to your bedroom. For example, if the room energy comes from the north, place the north direction of the Bagua right on the doorway and mark in the other seven areas. Ideal spaces are rectangular. Each side of the Bagua represents a particular part of life and when the energy centers of the Bagua extend beyond the space, or are missing for the space, it is an indication that the corresponding parts of life

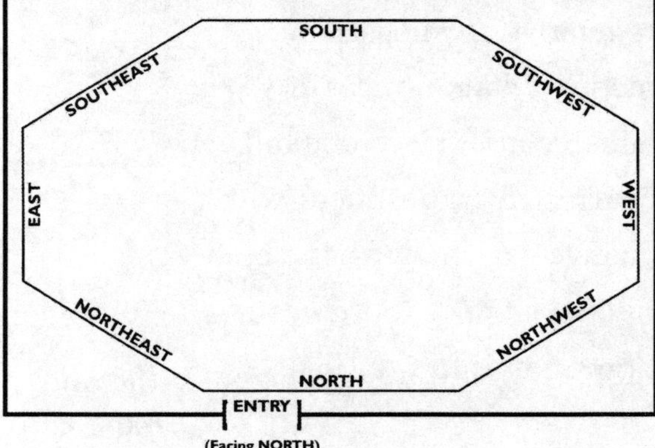

might also be dangling or missing. Then you would use "cures" like mirrors, paintings, houseplants, lights, flutes, on or next to the internal wall to stimulate the energy there. Where have you placed your bed, dresser, and maybe mirror? Please don't place the headboard on the bathroom wall; the bathroom's energy is negative on the bedroom since it is an area that deals mostly with pipes and wastewater. Keep the bathroom door closed most of the time. Please don't place a mirror opposite the bed. Your soul doesn't want to be shocked when you look in the mirror upon arising after a night's sleep.

Each of the nine areas, the eight directions plus the center, reflects certain characteristics and aspects of your life. Here is an example: you have serious financial problems. In your bedroom there are piles of magazines in the Southeast corner that you haven't gotten around to reading yet. Physical clutter like these piles adversely affects you and your chi energy currents. Remove the magazines completely from the money area. Also be sure to remove any negative pictures, bank notices of failed loans, or overdue bills. Making this adjustment will change over time whatever financial opportunities can now enter into your life.

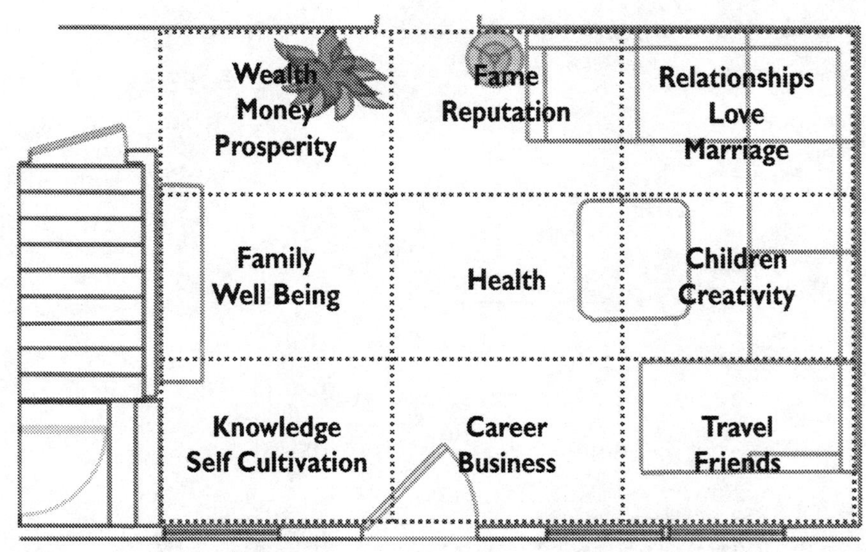

This living room floor plan has been divided into nine equal areas. Mark each to correspond to the Bagua's nine energy areas.

Your home is another layer of yourself and reflects what is going on for you and your family on many different levels. Use the Bagua to map each room and unblock the energy flow in each room and on all floors. Remember that blockages in the chi's flow will impede your family's progress in life.

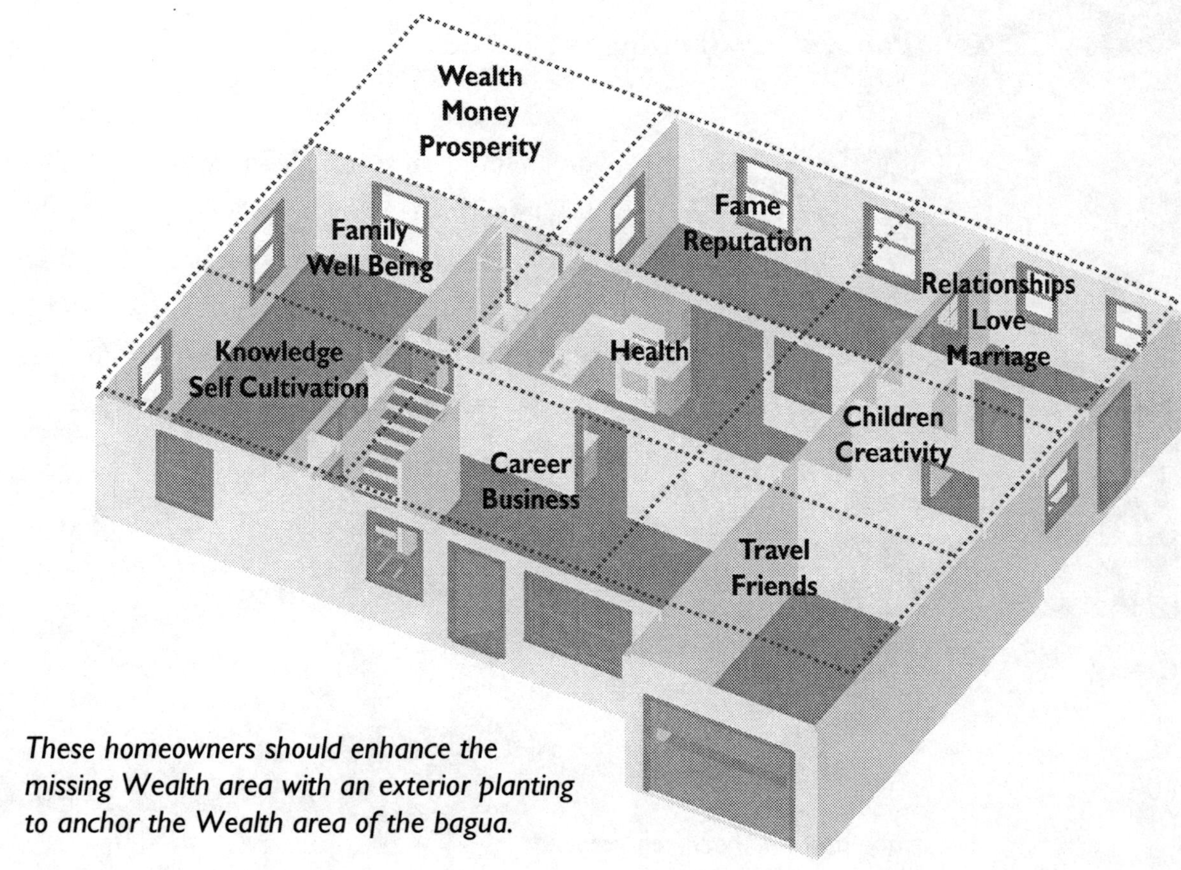

These homeowners should enhance the missing Wealth area with an exterior planting to anchor the Wealth area of the bagua.

Part 2: Awakening the Senses

Have you an office that looks like this…

Chaos is a problem that at times can be overwhelming. Just stop, breathe deeply, collect yourself, and when you have completed this book, you will have the tools to bring harmony and not stress into your lives, and your home will have the harmony and the energy to let you live in it the way you choose.

…or one that has been reorganized by the Feng Shui practitioner?

We know what pleases us when we rely on our intuition. We can make the decision whether or not to buy a particular house or condominium if we base our decision on the condition of the property, price, location, inspection report, and finances. We make decisions about what kind of furniture to buy, its shape, and color. But often we don't go along with our intuition, and that's when we need Feng Shui to help us create a family home that suits the complex and stressful life of every member. We want an environment where our home is safe and calm; where the family can retreat and share meaningful conversations.

This 13-year-old's desk and bookcase create a calm working environment.

Creating Positive Environments in Your Home

To create such an environment, you must ensure that the invisible energy or chi can move freely through your home without obstruction. For if anything impedes that easy flow, it will get between you and the life you desire. Stuff equals clutter, and clutter equals obstruction — get rid of what is unnecessary and keep only what you need and love. The process of throwing away creates space, lets chi move freely, and allows you to have in your lives what you and your family really want and need.

Eight aspirations in life correspond to the Bagua compass directions:

North: Career and Business 

Let us enter your home through the front door, also the entry point for currents of chi energy that moves as people walk through them. This energy current represents your career path as well as your journey through life. It represents ambition, where hard work is recognized as well as the progress that you make in your career. To maximize the flow of positive energy, the main entrance must be in good condition, with a freshly painted door, working doorbell, and adequate lighting. There should be no dead leaves and dirt on the outside or clutter of shoes, papers, or sports equipment on the inside. This area is associated with the direction of north, winter, the color black, and the time of midnight. It is also the Water element area. If you choose to boost the energy here, use water to energize the moving chi current and install a fountain, hang pictures of moving water, or set up a fish tank. Introducing the element of water will help you find your career path. In your office, be sure that the trash is emptied regularly, the computer is in good working condition, and your workbag, personal organizer, and your cell phone are on the desktop.

Northeast: Knowledge and Self Cultivation

The northeast has as its element Earth and corresponds with early spring, and periods of calm, stability, and knowledge. Without Earth in a room, we tend to drift or feel lethargic. You can add Earth with marble sculpture, pottery, rock gardens, earthly colors of gold, ochre, and yellow, candles, or leather items and plants.

The northeast corner of a living room.

East: Family and Well Being 东

The direction of east is the family relationships and community area of your life. It connects with the Wood element, to patience and courage, to energy in the early part of the day, sunrise, and springtime. The color green is associated with this area. Reinforce the close relationships you have with your partner and children, grandparents, and relatives by displaying family photographs of celebrations in wooden frames. Communicate with others by telephone, fax, or computer, keep new project files, and conduct community involvement projects in this area of your home. This area should also have two or more chairs to provide community seating. In order for the family to move forward in life, useless things from the past must be discarded. Pictures of past relationships that are no longer in your life should be removed.

Southeast: Wealth, Money, and Prosperity

The direction of the southeast reflects our relationship to money. That would mean your salary, money in the checking account, inherited money, and your definition of affluence. Wood is associated with money as well as the color green, early summer, and late morning. In this clutter free corner, if you wish to energize it (and most people would want more income), place round leaf plants, coins, and maybe some red flowers.

South: Fame and Reputation 南

The south is represented by the sun when it is hottest. This area is strongest in the middle of the day. Its season is summer, a time of promise and full growth. Its element is Fire and it corresponds with the qualities of intelligence, spirit, and understanding, and with the color red.

This living room provides ample comfort for good conversations and lively discussions.

Southwest: Relationships, Love, and Marriage

The direction of southwest is the relationship area and is associated with the Earth element, Indian summer, mid-afternoon, yellow, brown, and earth colors. When you and your family members are content, they are tuned into what they love and can feel happy. Family members know how to empower themselves and have a friendly family. Healthy plants, a desk and comfortable chair, an assemblage of gifts children have made for family members, and awards would be appropriate in this area.

West: Children and Creativity 西

The direction of west is the descendent or creativity area. This is the area associated with the Metal element, with happiness, hope, joy, the colors grey and silver, autumn, and glorious sunsets. This is the place of female energies, representing the children you want to have or nurturing the ones you already have. It is the area for personal creativity such as starting a new business plan or writing a book, for community involvement, church, and volunteer projects. Keep jigsaw puzzles, creative toys, games, healthy plants, and maybe a table with a chess set in this area.

Northwest: Travel and Friends

The direction of northwest is the wisdom, education and compassion area. Wisdom comes from being willing to learn from experience. It means getting the message, not just the facts. It also means the ability to empathize, thereby promoting meaningful relationships. Wisdom includes improving yourself as well as helping children meet their potential. This area is associated with the Metal element, late autumn, evening, and the colors blue and black.

The center of wisdom is located to the northwest of the entrance door. This is the area for neatly hung coats on coat hooks or a small welcoming table for keys and mail. A mountain, reflecting inner calm and peacefulness, is the symbol for wisdom.

Center: Health

The center of the Bagua is the health area, including physical, mental, and spiritual health. Because all of the chi currents meet here, this is a critical area of stability and balance for the family. Usually we look at it in a gathering room and it exists in all rooms of the family home. Like all rooms, this area must be in good condition, clean, and clutter free. It shouldn't be empty, but have a table with items that interest the family on it. An area rug with pattern and color in this location will bring forth vitality for the family.

A summary of the energy areas

Some areas of the Bagua can be impractical to implement. Here is a chart to help you with this dilemma:

SOUTHEAST **Wealth, Money, Prosperity** Helpful for being persistent, sensitive, and feeling positive, but can make you feel irritable and impatient. Increases the desire to be creative, imaginative, generate new ideas, seek harmony, communicate, and spread ideas. The symbol of wind makes it ideal for spreading ideas in a similar way to the wind spreading seeds.	**SOUTH** **Fame, Reputation** Helpful for being passionate, excited, generous, flamboyant, and dramatic, but at the same time, proud, hysterical, and self-centered. Increases the desire to be expressive, sociable, spontaneous, outgoing, get noticed, lead fashions, and be quick minded. This fiery chi energy is bright and colorful. It radiates energy.	**SOUTHWEST** **Relationships, Love, Marriage** Helpful for being caring, patient, and sympathetic, and conversely, dependent and jealous. Increases the desire to be practical, down to earth, consolidate, add quality, form long-term relationships, and be secure. The late summer represents the time of year when fruit and vegetables have stopped growing and are ripening. It is, therefore, the ideal energy for improving the quality of whatever you do.
EAST **Family, Well Being** Helpful for being enthusiastic, confident, assertive and, conversely, for feeling frustrated and angry. Increases the desire to start new projects, be alert, focus on details, get things right, analyze, be precise, and concentrate. The symbol of thunder gives this energy a loud, forceful edge, which is helpful for going out and making things happen.	**CENTER** **Health** This energy links all the eight directions. It does have an influence on the health of your body. As such it is an energy that can help you become the center of attention and attract people. It is the most powerful of all the chi energies and is, therefore, treated with respect.	**WEST** **Children, Creativity** Helpful for being romantic, content, and playful, and conversely, being depressed and pessimistic. Increases the desire to enjoy the pleasures of life, be wealthy, form new relationships, and be stylish and complete projects.
NORTHEAST **Knowledge, Self Cultivation** Helpful for being motivated, driven, and outgoing but, conversely, greedy and shrewd. Increases the desire to seize opportunities, win, compete, learn, and be decisive, clear-minded, and adventurous.	**NORTH** **Career, Business** Helpful for being sexual, spiritual, and independent, and conversely, isolated and aloof. Increases the desire to be flexible, find peace, study, develop oneself, improve health, be objective, and be different.	**NORTHWEST** **Travel, Friends** Helpful for being in charge, dignified, and responsible, but at the same time, authoritarian and arrogant. The desire is to feel in control, organize, plan ahead, find and be a mentor, be respected, and have integrity.

What is the Tao?

道 Another essential element in Feng Shui is the *Tao* (pronounced *Dao*). Tao is the "life force, the path taken by natural events and observable phenomena." It defines our relationship with nature and our surroundings. The principle of the Tao blends the energy or chi together with the concepts of yin and yang.

For example, every home needs a "heart": a gathering room for all the family connections—socializing, watching television or a movie together, snacking. This room is the life-supporting heartbeat for the family home. Incorporate in your gathering room comfortable furniture, an entertainment center, a calendar, a pencil and notepad next to the telephone, plants, and an area for reading material. Eliminate the clutter. Use the Feng Shui cures listed below to solve the imbalances of the chi and Tao.

The Tao should flow through your home like this stream meanders.

What is Yin and Yang?

阴阳 Yin and yang are complementary opposites. When the yin and yang are out of balance, a stressful life is often present and we must use Feng Shui tools to correct the imbalance. Yin and yang are evident in our lives whether we are asleep or awake. Yin is often considered inward, calm, and still. Less bright than yang, yin is often associated with female energy. Yang, on the other hand, is associated with male energy, is considered loud, varied sounds, bright lights, and bright colors. It is associated with an outgoing personality. Both yin and yang are necessary for harmony, and most of us prefer a blending of both to create the balance that we are all searching for in our lives.

When yin and yang are out of balance, stress is often the result. Correcting the imbalance restores harmony. The family room is where conversation, activity, television, and games happen in a yang environment. Frank Lloyd Wright often designed open living and dining rooms to be yang gathering rooms. We can only imagine what the atmosphere and conversations were like!

I choose to have bedrooms represent the yin characteristics for rest and private time. Here are different examples of a master bedroom.

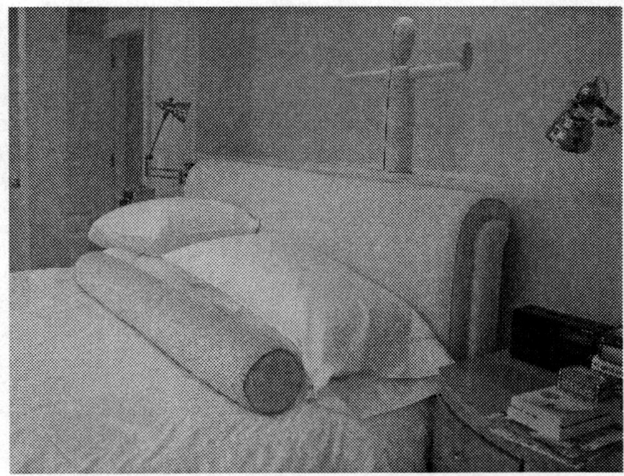

A minimalist approach to a master bedroom.

This master bedroom combines Feng Shui elements, color, texture, and light.

How to make your home more Yin:

- Add soft furnishings, such as upholstered chairs and sofas.
- Use rugs or carpeting made from a natural fiber such as wool.
- Hang natural-fiber curtains such as linen, cotton, or silk.
- Put large cushions on the floor for the younger members of the family.
- Avoid bright colors. Use cream, pale green, soft blue, or shades of peach or salmon in your color schemes.
- Use dimmer switches to control indirect lighting.
- Paint or plaster walls or use light wood paneling.
- Keep doors closed where possible to slow down the flow of chi energy.
- Play music that helps you relax.
- Use candles when possible.

Try these ways of increasing Yang in your home:

- Add metal objects, especially shiny ones.
- Use polished surfaces, such as a wooden table, stained hardwood, or tile floor.
- Choose shutters or wooden blinds instead of curtains: more chi energy will enter and leave the room.
- Use bright colors.
- Use bright lights, maybe halogen spots or track lighting.
- Direct spots on artwork or sculpture.
- Paint walls and ceiling off-white to reflect available chi energy back into the room.
- Remove clutter to allow chi energy to flow freely.
- Play music with a definite rhythm to promote more active sound waves.
- Use mirrors to reflect chi back into the room and speed up the flow of energy.

- Add bright, colorful, fresh flowers.
- Add plants with pointy or spiky leaves that allow for greater movement of chi energy.

As the sun rises in the east, the eastern and southern parts of your home will be vitalized by the sun's energy, raising the chi levels in those areas and increasing more yang. That makes the east side of your home suitable for activities that require more Yang. The west side of the house is more Yin. If you think you are too yin and want to raise your energy level, spend more time in a yang part of your house. In the winter, people often choose to do their activities in the morning in the east where they have more energy.

Feng Shui Cures

The Chinese developed cures, which Feng Shui practitioners continue to use to this day to remedy negative flows of chi energy. Here is a guide.

Feng Shui Cure	When to Use It	Where to Use It
Color	Use bright colors such as red, orange, and yellow to stimulate the stagnant, cluttered energy in a dark area or cupboard.	West
Lights, mirrors, clean and symmetrical crystals	Use these cures to deflect a sharp point, like a wall.	South
Metal chimes with hollow tubes, bells	Use these cures to activate energy. Hang them over clutter.	Northwest
Statues and rocks	Use these to slow down the energy that travels in a straight line; for example, in a long corridor leading to a cluttered area.	West
Fans and flutes	Use these to soften a sharp corner of a wall.	East
Music	Use to stimulate stagnant energy.	Northeast

Using Colors

We respond to color on many different levels, mostly unconsciously. How comfortable we are in an environment will be evidenced in our mood. The color of our dress will affect how others perceive us. If I wear a red suit to a meeting, others will perceive me as being strong and overpowering. That might not be my intention if I am on a sales call.

The light in a room will affect the color, might absorb it or reflect it. You can use different pigments of a color to create different illusions in the room. Different textures, different applications of the paint, or even wallpaper can be used to gain the desired effect you want to create the harmony and move the chi energy.

I tell my clients that if they are undecided what color green to use in an area, or any color, buy a quart of two different tints and apply them to some cardboard and tape the cardboard to the wall and look at the samples in daylight and at night time under artificial light. Then return to the paint shop with your decision and buy the paint.

Red: Red is stimulating and dominant. It is useful as an accent color. Please don't use it in a child's room, dining room, or kitchen. It is associated with warmth, prosperity, and stimulation.

Yellow: Yellow is associated with enlightenment and intellect; it stimulates the brain and aids digestion. It is suitable for hallways and the kitchen with its optimistic quality.

Green: Green symbolizes growth, fertility, and harmony. It is good to use it in a restful area like a library, bathroom, or bedroom.

Blue: Blue is peaceful and soothing and is linked to spirituality, contemplation, mystery, and patience. It is good to use it in bedrooms, dining rooms, and meditation areas for it also enlarges spaces.

Pink: Pink is linked to clear thinking. Use it in bedrooms for its association with romance and happiness

Purple: Purple encourages vitality and is impressive, dignified, and spiritual. It signifies passion and excitement in bedrooms, libraries, and therapy offices.

Orange: Orange is a powerful and cheerful color and encourages people to communicate. In large areas like living rooms or dining rooms, it encourages people to be happy and positive

Brown: Brown suggests stability and weight. It is a safe color when used in libraries and offices, maybe in the paneling.

White: White symbolizes beginnings, purity, and innocence. You can use a variation of white in the bathroom or the kitchen, so that it looks clean and fresh.

Black: Black is mysterious and independent. Its positive qualities are intrigue, strength, and allure or the opposites: death, dark, and evil. Yin is the blackness because it absorbs all colors. Black can be used in combination with white in the bathroom or kitchen.

Plant Guidelines

Plants are an important part of our home and play a major role as a cure in Feng Shui. They have different shapes, textures, and colors and add freshness to our home. They must be kept healthy, free of disease, shedding leaves, and dead flowers.

We categorize the plants that are yang by being upright with pointed leaves; they are useful in the south and in corners to move more energy. Round leaved plants with maybe drooping leaves are found to be more calming and yin energy, and are best placed in the north.

The jade plant has often been called the money plant; its leaves resemble coins and Metal energy. Plants with colorful blossoms will brighten up any area and increase Wood energy. Geraniums are easy to grow and, with their red blossoms, represent Fire energy. To induce the Water energy, you may put ivy or philodendron in water as it grows well in that environment. Earth energy is in pots of yellow flowered plants like chrysanthemum.

This display of plants with soft-edged leaves brings nature indoors to energize the occupants.

Plants can be used in the following ways:

- Move the energy in a recessed corner
- Bring life into a house
- Slow down the chi in hallways

- Move the Water energy excess in bathrooms
- Support the south area of the Bagua as well as enhance the east and southeast
- Add drama when lighting is directed from the floor on plants

More on Mirrors

Mirrors are an easy way to balance chi. Follow these guidelines.

- Don't place a mirror opposite the entry or door of any room because it will deflect the chi entering the room and encourage negative chi to remain. This situation can cause bad temper, crankiness, or emotional problems.
- Don't hang a mirror so that it cuts off your head.
- Don't hang a mirror so that it splits an image, reflects an angle, or magnifies a problem in a room.
- Don't place a mirror opposite the bed, because it will draw energy from you into the mirror. Don't even put a mirror above the dresser opposite the bed.
- Don't have a mirror in view upon awakening. Your soul should not be shocked as it views your appearance after sleep.
- Avoid cheap, inferior quality mirrors with distortions, black spots, chips, cracks, or scratches.
- Keep all mirrors clean. Dust on a mirror can cloud your emotions.

Using Your Senses

Chi, the force that vitalizes our life, is not elusive. We perceive it through our senses, by taking in the experiences from our environment.

Sight

With our eyes we perceive movement, light, and lines. The colors, patterns, and lines we see determine our emotional reactions. Colors that are dark and deep affect us more physically, while mid-range colors serve us spiritually. When planning the colors for rooms in your home, be mindful of the emotional response you want in that room. Light yellow is a good color to surround yourself with when mental clarity is needed to absorb information. Candles on the table will enhance a leisurely dining environment, whether used for family or with company. An atmosphere conducive to good conversation and relaxation promotes good digestion.

A balanced arrangement of furniture with shapes, patterns, textures, and lighting is what I would choose for everyone. Tables may have curved lines as opposed to sharp corners. This applies to chairs and sofas as well. If it's your choice to use pillows on a sofa, don't use too many; allow enough room for a person to sit comfortably with the pillows as an accent or for back support. You want your eyes to move around the room and perceive the right proportions of the furniture in relationship to the size of the room. You want to enter this room and engage in conversation and relax.

Hearing

Through sound we absorb energies that change the chi within us. Different musical rhythms, voices, electrical devices, fans, wind, and water all elicit different reactions in all of us as well as change the chi in a room. When you expect company for dinner, turn the stereo on and the television off.

Smell

Scents are particularly evocative of childhood and past experiences. I remember arriving at our grandparents' home on the water in Connecticut, inhaling the damp smell, and instantly feeling welcome. A home redolent of roasting chicken reminds you of mother's or grandma's cooking, of feeling welcome in a place you want to be. Specific scents like lavender, lemon, and mint assist in relaxation. Use aromatherapy to create a particular mood.

Touch

Physical contact with others is critical to our emotional well-being. Also important is the feel of fabric, whether clothing or upholstery. Cashmere feels softer than plain wool. Velvet, chenille, or silk upholstery fabrics are more comfortable than rayon, nylon blends, or horsehair. Fabrics, especially patterns on beds, should make each family member feel nurtured, sensuous, and relaxed.

Well-chosen prints, patterns, and textures bring rhythm and movement into the room environment. You can achieve the illusion of texture and incorporate colors into the room with the use of small patterns. I like to use patterns with swirls, leaf, and small flowers replicating nature. Stripes should be used carefully; their straight lines may cause tension in the room especially when used on vertical surfaces.

What do You Want Your House to Say?

Feng Shui adjustments can be layered for the best results. Use this approach when an issue is having a serious impact on your life or when you want results quickly. Layer improvements to the energy flow by adjusting a specific area, such as wealth, in three different locations in your home.

If money is a serious concern, find the wealth sector in different areas of your home. In those corners, place something that represents money to you. Use a healthy plant if you are trying to grow a healthy investment, a chime if you want to raise money in general, or a fountain to signify the cash flow you are looking for. Whatever you use, the adjustment must be appropriately suited to your taste. If it engages your intention, it will remind you what it is you are seeking.

Now locate the wealth area of your bedroom and make appropriate changes there as well. Use a different Feng Shui cure, like adding the rich colors of red or purple. Then add yet a third layer to your wealth intention by making an appropriate alteration to your desk. A bell, some bright flowers, or a $100 bill under a statue will support and enhance the adjustments you have made in the other parts of the house.

Be sure to prioritize the changes that you want. Once you have made adjustments by applying Feng Shui cures, you will be clear about your intention to change. All items will be in place to enhance the positive flow of chi energy. Let go of the outcome. You can't rush the results — they will follow the natural flow of events. Why not be ready to receive the adjustments to your life?

People that I have counseled have wanted new love relationships. I have told them to look at the southwest corner of their bedrooms; if there is a night table next to their beds, to make sure that it is clutter free. Then place a framed photograph of a couple that they like, perhaps parents or a sister with her husband or partner, and place a bud vase with two red flowers there. They were also to tell their network of friends that they want a new relationship. By making this request a priority, within a reasonable amount of time, they have told me that they are dating someone special. It's an amazing process that works for you if you believe it will.

Without leaving your home, you can begin to understand the rest of the world. Your perspective of life is filtered through your senses. By changing your environment, you change your perspective. If you have to filter through a lot of baggage like where you got that vase, from whom and when, to see what's happening, you cannot see clearly. Your world becomes heavy and does not allow you to be free. When you manage your affairs at home, you can be assured of managing them elsewhere: the control you exert over the physical space that you agreed to take care of helps you control the outer elements of your life. Once you are in control of your personal world, everyone in the outside world will notice the special person that you are.

Keep in mind that less is more, and make continual small changes in both your personal and outside world. Living with intention requires that your eyes be open and your mind discerning. Each object that you own requires your energy and time, and many possessions can become negative energy drains. You need to move each object, clean it, store it, water it, dust it, or provide whatever care it needs. Your energy gets diffused as it is spread out over many items. You begin not to see what you have. You often no longer connect with what you own. Your environment needs to speak to your intention in order for you to make the changes you want in your life. Objects in your home draw energy from you. Get rid of objects that you received from someone you don't like anymore. The goal is to have the objects in your space enhance your life, promote your creativity, and make you feel special and unique. You want a living room to be a study in balance and harmony, with large-scale, neutral-hued pieces serving as anchors for an array of accent objects, like sculpture, art, flowers, and craft items. Then when you are in the mood to change the look of the room, simply rearrange the smaller objects and you won't need to purchase anything new.

This room in New England accommodates the seasons with cozy fires in the winter and open doors to the porch in the spring, summer, and fall.

Part 3: Rooms in Your Home

The entrance to a house or apartment is an important determining factor in energy flow. It is the portal by which the chi enters, affecting everyone who lives within. Front and back doors should not be lined up or in view of each other. If that is the case, the energy of the chi will enter and then immediately leave out the back. If they are, add cures to the area like plants or furniture. All rooms should have adequate natural light to promote yang or life energy.

The front door should always open inward into an uncluttered foyer. Moving through this area, the chi is channeled throughout the rest of the home. The foyer should be well lit and the pathway to the rest of the home obvious. If there is a stairway, it should not face the front door. It should be straight, with wide shallow stairs, preferably carpeted. Add a cure here, like the wind chimes. The arrangement of levels and rooms should be as regular as possible to allow the energy to flow with ease.

Bedrooms opening up off the hallway are a good arrangement. They should be well lit with natural light. Bedroom ceiling can be flat, arched, vaulted, or domed, and not too high so that the chi can rise and move evenly. If not necessary, don't use ceiling fans as they interfere with the steady flow of the energy currents. Well-organized closets will keep clothes and accessories orderly and when you open your closet door, you will feel ease in selecting what you will wear for the day, or what you might need to purchase.

An office or study area should not have a door in direct line with an exit from the house. Keep the energy currents flowing. These are places for work, success, and prosperity.

The kitchen should be shielded from the front entrance; it is the heart of your home and should be protected from any entering negative energy. It should be regular in shape. The stove, which represents Metal, should not adjoin either a Water or a Wood element. Being next to Wood increases the danger of fire, while being next to Water produces a damp situation.

If possible, the garage should be separate. Because the movement of cars disrupts the flow of energy in the house, a separate garage prevents negative energy from spreading. No rooms for living, like a bedroom, living room, or kitchen, should be located above the garage. The garage area carries fumes, garbage cans, tools, and is often not orderly.

The best shape for a deck is circular. Hot tubs, too, should always be circular, with strong pillars for support.

Banners, flags, wind chimes, and mobiles—anything that moves in a breeze—activate and disperse lingering chi, as does gently flowing water and smoke from burning incense. These can be used at entryways or porches.

Statues of Buddha or goddesses, rocks or stones, and driftwood can affect the good chi when placed in an area of the Bagua that needs energizing.

The Master Bedroom

The placement of the bedroom within the house determines the status of its occupants. Decide whether you want the chi in the room to be restful or active, and plan accordingly. For restful chi energy, choose a bedroom in the back of the house away from the main street, and place the bed as far away from the entry to the house as possible. The bedroom is not the place for parties and entertaining, but a private area for the family members who sleep there.

The bedroom is especially appropriate for relationship enhancements. Place items around you that you love. Nothing should be broken or cracked. Remember your Bagua and pay attention to the southwest or relationship corner of the bedroom. Place romantic images there, including symbols of union and pairs of items like candles. Two rose quartz crystals in the southwest corner will enhance a loving relationship.

If you are currently in a relationship, or want to attract one, the bedroom should be your focus. Once it is the place you have romantically designed and clutter free, you will be comfortable in it and sleep more peacefully. Your life will become what you want. (1) Adjust the room according to the Bagua and Feng Shui cures. (2) This will improve the flow of chi. (3) You will feel better. (4) Your life will become what you want.

Your Bed

You use your bed when you are most vulnerable, tired, or sick. It is the recipient of good and bad dreams. Because beds have memories, when you begin a new relationship in the same bed, be sure to buy new linens. If you change your life, you can rearrange the furniture as well. When you start

something new, reevaluate the "feel" of the room.

It is advisable not to place the head of the bed against the bathroom wall. If this is impossible and you must face the bathroom, place a mirror on the wall opposite the toilet to symbolically move it. Remember to keep the bathroom door closed.

Elevate the mattress of the bed about three feet off the floor and place it on a frame and castors. Clear clutter from under the bed and allow an air gap. Items stored under the bed may cause you to have restless nights as well as interrupted sleep. If your mattress or futon is placed directly on the floor, you are likely to have backaches.

I advise couples or parents to have a solid headboard to help bind a relationship, to reinforce their strength in making family decisions, and anchor the bed and its occupants. Generally, it is advisable to have a tightly secured headboard made out of wood, an element good for nurturing, creativity, and procreation. Its sturdiness has a yin quality conducive to sleep. For a softer look, choose a padded headboard with a wood frame. A metal frame is good for a person who is charming and conciliatory as well as firm in morals and ethics. Headboards should be backed by a wall, not windows that can make the occupants feel insecure and let drafts in to the room.

Footboards should match headboards. If you choose to have a footboard, make it the height of the mattress. If there is no footboard, place a multifunction chest or bench at the foot of the bed. You can place the bedspread on it or even sit on it.

Different types of beds have specific effects on chi energy. Sleigh beds, for example, are confining. A waterbed will increase your ability to attract friends. A cotton futon on the floor is ruled by the element Fire, which makes it a good bed for meditation and thought, not for sleeping.

Adding the following colors to the bed will add the related element regardless of its material:

GREEN	YELLOW	RED	WHITE or GREY	BLACK or DARK BLUE
⇩	⇩	⇩	⇩	⇩
Wood	Earth	Fire	Metal	Water

To follow the natural flow of energy, place the head of the bed in the north and its foot in the south. If you choose to have your headboard in the west, or counter to the movement of the earth; you should sleep alone. Never place a bed at an awkward angle to accommodate a direction. It is better to have a clear view of the entry from the bed. The symmetry of tables and lamps at each side of the bed should be perfect, with the same furnishings so that both partners consider themselves as equal. An open canopy bed without any excess fabrics gives a very pleasant effect.

The foot of the bed should never point to the door. This placement can drain your energy, and you'll wake up tired. In China, it is considered the "mortuary position" because coffins are placed in that position when awaiting collection! You should also avoid placing the bed under a beam, especially at right angles to it. It symbolically divides the couple.

Keep the pathway from the bed to the bathroom clear to prevent accidents in the dark. Computers, bookcases, a treadmill, or extraneous equipment in the bedroom may cause chronic illness, difficulty making decisions, and an inability to start on a new project. The chi must be able to flow unimpeded through the bedroom, around, above, and below. Make sure the bed can be accessed from both sides, allowing equality in a relationship.

Shelves should not be placed on the headboard; shelves are places to collect clutter of things to fall upon you. Don't install a wall of mirrors in the bedroom, or a mirror large enough to see yourself first thing in the morning.

Avoid too many fresh plants in the bedroom. Instead, put fresh flowers in clean fresh water on the dresser or night table.

Master Bedroom Closet Tips

1. Take all clothing, shoes, belts, and other items of apparel out of the closet and place them on the bed to sort through. Check the condition of the clothes and separate them into piles: keep, clean, recycle, discard, resell, or give away.
2. Make sure that the clothes that return to the closet all fit you *now*.
3. Sort your clothes into groups when returning them to a clean closet: skirts, slacks, suits, dresses, sports outfits.
4. Get rid of shoes that don't fit, that may cause discomfort, or are out of style.
5. Keep your handbags clean and in order. A cluttered and overloaded handbag reflects the same condition in your life. Get rid of handbags you no longer want or use.
6. Make a list of the clothing, shoes, and accessories you can now look forward to purchasing.

Removing clutter from your closet and elsewhere in your home may help you find a partner, either in business or in a personal relationship, or improve your relationship with a current partner. By clearing clutter, you symbolically make space for that person to come into your life.

The Kitchen

We need both food and chi to live, and the quality of the food that we prepare in the kitchen helps determine the activity of our spirit. That makes the kitchen a very important room: it provides your family with life, security, and comfort. The kitchen symbolizes the benefit of serving others and ourselves and allowing ourselves and our children to mature. Remember the wonderful smells that came from the kitchen of your childhood? The food you smelled nourished your soul as well as your body. The kitchen is one of the most important rooms in the house, providing the means to nourish both our bodies and our chi.

Kitchen for a large family designed with all the Feng Shui elements.

The location of the kitchen is not as important as its condition. It must be well lit and airy. Add overhead or under-the-cabinet lights if necessary, and paint it a light color. Food preparation areas like countertops must be clear of clutter.

The kitchen doorway should not be directly apparent from the front door of the house. When you stand at the sink or stove, you should be able to see the kitchen entry. Knowing who comes in and out will prevent feelings of insecurity. If necessary, place a shiny tray or a mirror behind the sink or stove to reflect the doorway.

If the kitchen faces the living room or bathroom, keep those rooms closed or use screens or plants to separate them. The kitchen is the heart of our homes; we want the chi to linger there.

Stoves provide the family with food, the key to health and chi. Gas ovens and stovetops are preferable to electric because they have the focal point of a flame. Keep the stove clean and the burners uncovered. In Feng Shui, cooking is synonymous with money. A reflective device that doubles the burners will increase your cash flow. Create a separation between the sink and the stove, maybe with a counter. Water from the sink destroys the fire of the stove.

Make sure that all appliances are in good working order. Drips and leaks cause resources to drip away. Knives should be kept in drawers because they send out cutting chi. Don't let garbage pile up, or all kinds of psychic garbage will accumulate as well. Even dirty dishes are unacceptable clutter. Because the kitchen is where the chi is channeled into the body, always keep this room clean, clear, and in good working condition. Then you'll be cooking!

Wooden kitchen cabinets are best. Organize your cabinets as follows:

1. Keep only pots, pans, dishes, and glasses that are chip free and in good condition. Surfaces on pans should be clear and clean.

2. Use open-weave divider compartments in your cutlery drawers for easy maintenance.
3. Wrap open food in plastic or close bags with large clips.
4. Group and organize items by category: baking products, noodles, rice, unexpired canned goods, snacks, cereals, teas, sweeteners, and seasonings.
5. Periodically check all wheat products for bugs.
6. Make a list of items that need replacement.

The Dining Room or Breakfast Area

The dining area plays an important role in your family's life. It is a place for family members to come together, sit in a consistent place, communicate, interact, and resolve conflicts. Sitting together for whatever time is available will make life better for everyone in the family. A free exchange of ideas, activities, and beliefs will foster children's growth and development. A dining room is for dining only: the table should not be used for long-term work-related projects.

Dining on home-cooked foods prepared in a kitchen that has the right flow of energy will nurture all family members, including the cat and dog. Even food brought in from an outside source and served on plates is acceptable in our busy lives. A table set with a centerpiece, candles, and a sense of style encourages respect and love.

It is best if there are two doors or windows into the dining room, hopefully on adjacent walls, for the chi energy currents to keep active. A crystal chandelier provides energy flow as it plays with light.

Place the table in the center of the room and not under a beam; with enough room around it for circulation. The table should be wood, preferably round or oval, to promote interaction and interchange of ideas. Provide four, six, or eight chairs. If there are only one or two chairs, don't expect company—no one will come.

Here are some guidelines for harmonious dining:

- Choose comfortable chairs for all family members according to their age.
- Always have an even number of chairs at the table.
- If possible, diners should not have their backs to the door or windows.
- If possible, mom should sit in the **southwest** area and dad in the **northwest**.

The Family Room or Gathering Room

The west, north, or south quadrants of the house are good locations for television, DVD, computers, and electronic games. Divide the room into activity areas according to noise level, separating noisier pastimes from quieter ones: reading, puzzles, card games. Make sure that areas that need light have plenty. Place a table and lamp next to a chair and ottoman for reading. Organize CDs, movies, art supplies, games and books, lining up the books in one direction. You can add a small area for healthy green plants, a fish tank, or a fountain.

The more the chi can move around the room without encountering piles of old newspapers and magazines, the better family life will become. Removing clutter will also eliminate confrontations and difficult situations.

The Library or Home Office

Remember that the chi energy field extends outside your body; it is influenced by your environment and especially your office. Placing yourself in the most favorable chi energy field for the goals you wish to achieve requires a careful assessment of the energy in your office.

Where you sit when you work is of primary importance in determining the chi energy you are exposed to. The shape, color, and materials of office furniture also affect the ambient chi energy. Wooden desks with rounded corners, as well as a round conference table, are more conducive to creativity and interaction.

The desk acts as a command center for the family, where bills are paid and receipts, checkbooks, and important documents stored. A comfortable chair of appropriate height should be in good condition. Illuminate your work surface well, focusing the light directly on the materials on your desk.

The surface of the desk should be organized, clean, and orderly. Desk clutter will cause problems in your life: inability to complete projects, inefficiency, and confusion of family or personal goals. Keep bills out of sight. Entering the room to face a pile of debt is more than a bit discouraging.

Organize desk drawers:

- Designate a specific purpose for each drawer and keep similar items together: pens, pencils, staples, tape, envelopes, stationery, postcards, and stamps.
- Arrange containers in the drawers to hold paper clips, rubber bands, staples, rubber stamps, and computer supplies.
- Keep the organization simple for easy retrieval and continued neatness.

You should be able to see both door and office from your desk. Your desk is the seat of power, the location of maximum control, concentration, efficiency, and even authority. If your desk has a family history, be sure that it is an empowering one. Don't dissipate energy by spending a lot of time looking out of the window daydreaming.

Organize files in your desk, credenza, or file cabinets. Arrange reference materials neatly on bookcases. Set up a conference area with the current client account files awaiting attention. (Two types of offices are combined in this discussion: a professional home office and a command center for the entire family. And why are current client files kept in the conference area?) Don't block the flow of chi around your desk and credenza with books and folders on the floor or under the desk.

Carpeting or rugs, subtle in color, must be in good condition. Furniture should also be clean and in good repair. Fabrics on upholstered furniture should be solid or have a small pattern. Avoid overpowering furniture that takes up too much space. Place heavy furniture like credenzas and file cabinets along the wall, freeing up the path to the door. A minimalist approach to the design and placement of offices and furniture is the most successful one.

Photographs and degrees should be placed on one wall; artwork of landscapes, animals, botanicals, or special places visited on another. Well-cared-for plants with rounded leaves enhance the environment.

When husband and wife share the office, they should each communicate their needs and the best ways to coexist in the space. Both should cooperate in keeping the office organized and uncluttered.

Teenagers' Rooms

Teenager's rooms generally are very individual expressing their loves, their hurts and their angers as they grow into adults. These rooms are their private place in the family's home and they change over and over again as they leave their teens. We as parents try to have their beds in an auspicious position and introduce them to Feng Shui, which they may come to regard as a help when they encounter the usual trials of growing up. These rooms might be multi functional as they are used for study, entertaining friends, and sleeping. It is wise for the teenager not to have a television in their room, and for them to be encouraged to watch shows and films in the family room. When offering advice or support to teenagers, be sure that it is in the form of positive support.

Children's Rooms

Children's rooms should be simple and cozy, full of objects that offer possibilities for play and imagination as well as sleep. If your children sleep well, they can be delightful family members where harmony and love succeed. Place the crib or bed so that the children have a view of the door. Never place the child's headboard against a window. Rooms with dark corners which house strange shapes and cast shadows on the wall can prove disturbing for young children with vivid imaginations or who use every excuse not to go to sleep alone. Closet doors should be closed so no one lurks in the closet. Often a nightlight works to calm a child's anxieties.

Toddlers at play with age-appropriate toys.

The surroundings must be flexible: as children grow and change, so should their room. Paint and wallpaper color and images should be calming and restful to promote peaceful sleep. Don't block the flow of chi energy by hanging objects over the crib or storing them underneath. Provide adequate storage for clothes and toys, and teach toddlers to clean up and put toys away. Toys should be current ones that they play with now; you can recycle unused new toys by keeping them in the closet out of the way until you see it's time for different ones.

- Install a mirror on the closet door to help your child develop a sense of self.
- Position a light switch at a lower level so children can reach it to turn the light on and off.

Your children should have some control over how their rooms are decorated. Let them develop the decision-making process so important in later life.

Bathrooms

The bathroom is a personal space where we spend private time first in the morning and last thing at night. This area has an unnerving capacity for clutter. Here's what I would recommend to clear it out:

1. In the medicine cabinet, discard all expired prescription medications.
2. Throw out all half-used creams and lotions that are no longer your favorites.
3. Discard bits of soap and used-up toothpaste tubes, as well as any product or item your family no longer needs.
4. Keep environmentally safe bathroom-cleaning products only under the sink.
5. Install a shelf for extra storage space, including items like toilet paper, tissues, and hair dryers.
6. Use drawer dividers to keep makeup and nail-care items organized and neat.
7. If you are lucky enough to have a bathroom closet, organize it for the storage of specific items: different-sized towels, bedroom sheets, toilet paper, etc.
8. If space permits, use baskets to store small rolled-up towels.
9. Keep an eye out for decorative storage items. Look for a handsome wastebasket as well.
10. Keep the laundry hamper in the bathroom if at all possible.

Finally, make sure that the bathroom mirror always sparkles. A handsome picture on the wall facing the door is also a good distraction.

Storage Areas

Organize your garage and attic. Even though it's out of sight, clutter in these areas affects the inhabitants of the house just as much as clutter in the house itself. Here are a few tips for organizing storage areas:

1. Mark all stored boxes with their contents and the date you put them in storage.
2. Compile an inventory for easy retrieval.
3. Seal boxes tightly to keep out dust.
4. Store boxes in a dry place or on pallets.
5. If you have no future plans for the items you are storing, get rid of them.

Feng Shui in the Classroom

An environment that encourages teaching and learning.
Courtesy of Bay Farm Montessori Academy, Duxbury MA.

Feng Shui in the classroom, where children spend so many hours of their lives, is closely related to Feng Shui in the home. We want our children to have the best environment and energy flow for learning wherever they are. Children's investigation of life is shaped by the content of the physical world about them— the furnishings, artwork, flooring materials, and lighting of the classroom. In the classroom, all of a child's senses should be stimulated and enthralled.

The principles of Feng Shui reveal how an early childhood environment can constrain or expand a child's coping skills and approach to many life situations. For example, the amount of natural and artificial light and motion in a classroom can make a difference in how a child experiences the space. If a carpeted area has a pattern showing a lot of motion, children may have distractions that affect their behavior and learning. If the rest area in the classroom has a red carpet, the color represents fire and stimulation, thereby not encouraging naps. Why not choose blue, which is calming?

The arrangement of the classroom is important and must allow the chi energy to travel in all areas for the children to keep their attention span on the work, concentrate, and complete the work in a timely manner. Teachers need to have the confidence to teach and students need to have the intent to learn.

I know a teacher in junior high school, who has plants as well as decorative water fountains in his classroom. He finds that it keeps the students calm and at ease in a chaotic school and other teachers like to meander into his classroom.

Part 4: Clearing Clutter

Feng Shui practitioners believe in finding a balance between the universal forces of yin and yang. These opposing forces are in constant motion, and the friction between them creates the flow of positive energy through the various age levels in life. Because all forms of energy are related, changing the energy on one level will produce corresponding changes on others. Balancing the life force around you can result in improved health, increased income, and the fulfillment of your other desires.

Yin: tranquil and intuitive

Yang: energetic and active

Clutter is closely related to yang, and yang corresponds with male, aggressive energy. You feel tired, listless, and disorganized if the energy around you has been stimulated by too much clutter. Arguments can result; problems arise. Removing clutter is a first step toward achieving balance and allowing chi energy to flow though your space and life.

What is Clutter?

Clutter comes in many shapes and sizes. Some is in the form of outgrown clothing and shoes, articles in need of repair, items beyond repair that should be replaced and discarded, outgrown toys and books, torn linens, old tax information and receipts, newspapers, magazines, books, and bags of every description. Many of these are items you save "just in case" but never use.

Another form of clutter is of the sentimental rather than the "just in case" kind. Are your drawers still full of mementos you kept after your divorce? Sell the jewelry, give it away, or have it redesigned exactly to your liking. Burn photographs, cards, or letters from your former spouse. A bonfire is a good way to clear negative energy quickly and give you a new sense of freedom.

People refuse to clear clutter for a variety of reasons. What's your excuse?

"It's too daunting."

"The area has gotten out of control."

"I need everything and I know where everything is."

"I might need this one day."

"I'll be able to fit into this suit once I lose a few pounds."

Why do you hang on to things? Because of a fear of letting go in your life you have clutter. Your possessions form a barrier against the outside world or you might not be able to get rid of a gift that you dislike for sentimental reasons. Make a commitment to unload it and restore the balance in your life.

Clutter can have a major, and negative, impact on the family dynamic and the energy in your household. Look at the Bagua in your home: how does it reflect your life? If chi is not free to flow, it's time to UNCLUTTER. Restoring harmony will give you the motivation to clean out the worst areas.

Twelve Good Reasons to Clear the Clutter from Your Home or Workplace

Once you UNCLUTTER, you will be able to:

1. Simplify and organize your life.
2. Move through life with more ease.
3. Feel lighter and find it easier to attain goals.
4. See new opportunities and possibilities.
5. Have extra space to live and work.
6. Find items more easily, with less frustration.
7. Feel free to invite guests at any time without worrying about the mess.
8. Have conversations where everyone can hear and be heard.
9. Think about new purchases on a need versus want basis.
10. Give things away to others in need or to sell them on eBay.
11. Make more funds available for bills, vacations, or nurturing activities.
12. Stop holding back from realizing your desires and being stuck. Moving forward in life—that's what we all want.

Checklist: Where's the Clutter?

End the stagnation of airflow and energy! Read the following list and check off the areas where you need to get to work with an organized plan.

- ❐ 1. Entrance to your home: inside, outside, and behind the door
- ❐ 2. Hall table and drawers
- ❐ 3. Coffee table, end tables
- ❐ 4. Den or family room, including bookcases and storage cabinets
- ❐ 5. Home office filing cabinets and desktop
- ❐ 6. Dining room table, sideboard, and corners
- ❐ 7. Kitchen table, cupboards, drawers; pantry
- ❐ 8. Bedroom floors, closets, dresser drawers
- ❐ 9. Bathroom storage area
- ❐ 10. Linen closet
- ❐ 11. Basement storage space
- ❐ 12. Attic storage space
- ❐ 13. Garage storage space
- ❐ 14. Car interior—and clean the exterior, too!

Time to Clear it Out

Here's a plan of attack:

1. Begin with small areas: dresser drawers, a closet, a corner of the room.
2. Make a plan: a list of area to unclutter, a specific time to tackle the job, whom to call upon if you need help. You enlist the help of a friend, music blaring and windows open to allow fresh chi to enter with new energy.
3. Have plenty of containers: boxes, garbage bags, and strong shopping bags. Label each one: repair, recycle, trash, file, store, or sell.
4. Sort through the possible choices of what to do with each item: the most difficult part of the job, but you need to do it. Trust yourself to make the right decision when you get rid of items—there are no wrong choices.
5. Remove the bags from your home once your day's work is complete.
6. Clean the area thoroughly right after removing the clutter. You can even use incense or aromatherapy to assist in the cleansing process.
7. Consult a professional if all else fails. Professionals with no emotional attachment to your possessions provide more than design expertise—they will also be able to point out why you don't need an item any more.

Tomorrow or the next time is another day. It gets easier each time you repeat the process of removing clutter. Keep your goal in mind: to create a new space for freedom and happiness.

The Master Bedroom—a good place to start

I like to begin in the master bedroom because that is the area of your home where you spend the most time. The bedroom is a sanctuary for family relationships: a place for partners to talk on all levels of their relationship; for children to come in for reassurance, a goodnight hug, or a snuggle.

The quality of your sleep determines the quality of your day and affects all the members of your family. Clear under the bed, the night tables, and all corners. Remove laundry baskets sitting in the corner of the room. Recycle piles of newspapers and magazines that you haven't gotten around to reading in the past month.

Organize everyday clothing, sports attire, shoes, handbags, hats, and belts neatly in the closet. Double-hanging clothes are a wonderful way to maximize closet space. Choose the hangers that work for you. Consider installing hooks for chains or belts. Use all vertical space in the closet even if you need a ladder to reach the top shelf—it's a good place to keep out-of-season items or clothing for specialized sports activities like horseback riding. If clothes need cleaning or repair, put them in an area for action.

If you have no clue how to go about organizing your closet space, call in a specialist to help you evaluate your needs and then do the redesign work.

Move on to the Children's Rooms

The bedroom is the only room that is designated exclusively for the child. More than a sleeping area, it is a safe, secure place for children to express their individual nature and have fun with toys, books, and soft sculpture. In their own sanctuary kids can explore activities, do their homework, and have friends over to play, or enjoy time alone. Whether located near their parents' bedroom or some distance away, the bedroom is a personal space where children can find their inner voice.

Children creating crafts – future artists at work…

All your children's possessions should be put away in drawers, closets, chests, or bookcases. The closet is a good place for shelving, a laundry basket, and hooks for pajamas and other items. Clutter on the floor—stuffed animals, school papers, sports equipment, dirty clothes—creates unbalanced energy. Teach your children to UNCLUTTER, and set an example for them. They will learn to organize themselves, reduce frustration, stop wasting time on disorganized activity, and be ready when they're supposed to be. The balance between yin and yang energy will be available to your child in a clutter-free room.

Make a Commitment to End Clutter

Uncluttering is one of the best ways to reorganize your life and find balance. Once you have gotten rid of all the items that contribute to clutter, you will have a clearer picture of yourself, who you are, and who you want to be. The chi will flow unimpeded through all of your Bagua areas once they have been cleared. And you will notice that emotional clutter disappears with the physical. You can begin dreaming—and working toward the life of your dreams.

You probably learned to save and keep during childhood. As you approached adulthood, college, your first apartment, you continued the process. But too many possessions slow down energy. Clutter affects finances, health, and relationships, whether on a real or subconscious level. So make a long-term commitment to keep fewer material belongings.

More good news: if you are looking for a partner in a business or personal relationship, clearing the clutter will make room, both physically and emotionally, for someone to come into your life. Now doesn't that sound good?

Part 5: Parenting Tips *(and not related to Feng Shui)*

Parenting involves the creation of an internal intention to focus on what there is for you to love about your children, and expressing your love in different ways. It includes clearing out the clutter of how we ourselves were raised and creating who we are as an authentic expression of our own love for children. It is important to use chaos and order for optimal creativity, and to tap into our own wisdom about developmental capacities of children, thereby upgrading our own skills and capacities as caregivers. We as parents are constant role models, our children's first and most influential guide to thriving as individuals. What we say and do have great meaning and power to our children, who constantly have us under observation.

Parenting and the Bagua

The nine essential principles of courage, stillness, joy, receptivity, synchronicity, integrity, strength, gratitude, and connection should affect everything we do as we raise our children and prepare them to flourish and succeed. I have found the Bagua to be a clear guide to parenting, and have often referred to Feng Shui and the Bagua for tips in solving my clients' and my own parenting dilemmas.

Generosity and gratitude come from the heart. Your children learn these qualities from you, constantly and intently observing how generous you are to yourself, how you love yourself, how you receive gifts, words of praise, and caresses, and how generous you are in giving praise and acceptance. How you physically show your love—rocking, cuddling, and caressing your child, establishing a wonderful bedtime routine—is important.

Children watch you to learn about honesty and kindness to others. It's important for them to hear you tell the truth, apologize when you are at fault, and offer forgiveness to others. How you show anger with words or rage affects your children deeply, teaching them to do the same.

Sisters happily at play in the park.

WHEN you communicate with friends and family on the telephone is important. Don't talk on the telephone at mealtimes or when you are in the car with your children, dropping them off or picking them up after school. Your children want your attention at these times.

When your children tell you of a situation at school or play that has affected them negatively, it is important to listen to them completely and not react. They need to be heard first. You can ask them questions and provide solutions and a wise perspective, ultimately generating a resolution to the problem that you can both agree upon. Do this important communication at home in the room that best suits this serious conversation and encourages the speaking and listening. Many parents make the mistake of trying to have a serious conversation in the car, while driving and with the cell phone ringing; I would say that this is a chaotic environment.

Children thrive with limited choices and learn the beginnings of independence when requested to make choices like what to have for lunch or what color shirt to wear. If everything in the closet is current and in good repair as requested in Feng Shui, then there is no problem what your child chooses. Clear limits and boundaries must be set to teach children what can and can't be done and the consequences of disobeying your rules. However, we don't want always to dominate children and put them in the wrong.

Children also learn about promises from you. Not keeping your promises shows a lack of integrity and is difficult for children to understand. It will affect them forever. If you promise in the morning to take them to the mall after school to purchase a birthday gift for a friend, do it. Keep your word. If unforeseen circumstances prevent you, renegotiate the promise. Otherwise, your integrity will be suspect once you break the agreement. Running late in our hectic and overscheduled lives is an unfortunate reality; but being late to meet a child, husband, or friend does constitute a broken agreement and lack of integrity. Thoughtfully negotiating an agreement that you will be able to keep will work in the relationship. Children learn from our intentions and they observe how some people can get angry and others learn to ignore the parent's lateness.

Feng Shui helps us understand how the colors, shapes, scents, tastes, sounds, and smells surrounding us affect our emotions, imagination, and relationships with others and ourselves. It gives us the tools for developing our children's spirit, mind, and body to their highest potential. Your children's senses are open and receptive, just waiting to be stimulated. A child uses sensory experience to absorb the outside world and make decisions. Because all activities take place surrounded by chi, creating an environment that enhances energy flow will help your children develop and flourish. Applying the Bagua will help you evaluate how your family feels and create an environment that will make everyone feel better.

Caring for Yourself: An Essential Part of Parenting

Children look to us to be their guides through life. They watch us to learn honesty and kindness to others and how we run our own lives. Children watch us make choices of what we do with our daily life, what is on our calendar while they are at school and are we going to do the necessary errands and phone calls to support their busy after school schedules. We must take care of our own health and make sure that our homes reflect the Feng Shui balance and harmony necessary to remove stress and tension.

Do we take time out to do something nice for ourselves during the week? Do we pursue our passion in conversation with another, do we meet another for coffee after the kids are dropped off at school, do we go for a walk with a friend for exercise and socializing, do we plan a spa visit or a pedicure once a month, do we arrange or organize birthday parties for our friends, do we organize dinners for friends who are sick or who have suffered a family loss, or plan a movie date with a friend; I don't want you to forget that you can schedule a date with your husband, wife or partner on a regular basis and line up the babysitter in advance. These are a few of the ways that honoring yourself will give you new energy to deal with the children… Children will thrive if you can have a smile on your face and inside awareness that parenting and caring for yourself are compatible.

Your Infant

I hope that parents are able to provide a secure, safe, and clean bed for their infant. Sleeping in their own bed is the very first step toward a child learning that the world is for them to discover and how parents handle the putting-to-bed routine, will affect the parent and child's early relationship.

It is important for parents to realize the importance of holding their children whenever the opportunity arises. The physical interaction between parent and child begins before birth, a process we often refer to as "attachment parenting." A caretaker should hold the child in the same loving manner. This physical interaction has lasting effects on children. When they know and feel what caring is, they have a good chance of themselves becoming caring and empathetic adults. Often children who are not attached to a parental figure are the ones involved in violence as adolescents.

Nursing a child is a special privilege, building a strong bond between mother and child. If you are bottle-feeding, be sure to hold your child. This is not a time to multitask. Concentrate on relaxing with your baby. It is unwise to force your child to eat when he is at an adequate weight. Children will usually stop drinking or as toddlers they will pick the healthy foods that their body requires. When preparing food and presenting it, do it with love and make it look appetizing and appealing.

Pacifiers, thumb sucking, and security blankets are transitional objects. In the absence of parents or the usual caregiver, they provide needed security.

Crawling is an essential activity that balances both sides of the brain. All children must go through this important stage. It is a way for babies to discover their first bit of independence. Make sure that there is no clutter in the area where you put you child down on the floor. Follow the lead of your child and get down on the floor too. We sometimes call this "rug time," with parent and baby on the same level for communication. It is reported that children who don't experience crawling are often dyslexic. Children who learn to move with their body often have better balance and coordination than those who don't.

At bedtime children should be encouraged to sleep in their own crib. The crib should have bumpers, a special blanket, and maybe a stuffed animal. Don't crowd the crib with objects. Chi energy must circulate. Place the crib so your baby can see the door. The head of the crib should not be against a bathroom wall or under a window. Include a rocking chair in the bedroom, and relax in it with your baby before bedtime.

Develop your toddlers' senses with play. Give them water, clay, blocks, and metal with no sharp edges. Boxes that toys come in are a fun toy in themselves. Sitting in front of the television is a bad habit that does nothing to develop the child's brain. Whenever possible, make eye contact with your toddler, whether you approve of a behavior or not. With eye contact, you're less likely to end up scolding.

The Importance of Family Meetings and Giving Children Guidelines

It is obviously important for your children to know that you love them. From love they get self-esteem. Equally important is for them to know that you know that they love you. Children want to receive and deliver love. A child is constantly investigating and accepting the way things are and must receive parental guidance at the appropriate age, reinforced with positive actions and words. Discipline and structure are what children need and want, and saying "no" at the appropriate times is a gift you give your children.

Be aware that it is important to know that there is a gap between loving and having full control of children's lives. Move away from total responsibility to allow them to flourish. Only when you listen to your child will you know where they are in the gap. Don't be too quick to give ground. Once you give it, you can't take it back.

Your children are not you. You won't be able to change who you were at age seven through your children. Parents may feel guilty when they are involved with work and organizations and associations outside the home. Include your children in these experiences by sharing them. Explain what you did, what happened at the meeting you attended. Obviously, pitch your explanation to the age and level of understanding of each child. This way, children know that mom and dad are out there making a difference. Sharing and learning is critical.

Parents should discuss and agree on issues prior to setting the "house rules" that will inevitably be challenged by the children. Be what you say, and be consistent. That's how children learn their values. Don't say anything that you are not going to do. Threats don't work and are only a test and will backfire. Carry through as a responsible parent. Children want to know boundaries and they will test them to know that they are really there.

Parents must be available to their children. Their relationships with their children will inevitably affect how the children will relate to their peers and other adults. Listening is the critical factor in learning where children are in their relationships.

How the parents treat each other will be the models of how the children will expect to be treated by their future partners. Discussions and disagreements are healthy if they are handled in a respectful manner. Conflicts resolved in this manner will train the children in how to handle conflicts in their own lives without resorting to displays of anger or outbursts of violence.

Parents' displays of affection in the home teach children how to interact with their partners later in life. Expressing affection is a sign of security in the parents' relationship, which makes children feel more secure. The best thing that parents can do for their children is to show respect for each other. If there is no affection or maybe the affection "is out," look at the southwest corner of your bedroom and living room and see what might be blocking the chi energy currents and correct the area with cures.

Smart Tips for Parents When Hiring a Nanny

There are five phases in the nanny-hiring process: defining your needs, initial phone interview, face-to-face interview, checking references, and trial period.

1. **Define your needs:** Know thyself! Determine exactly what your family needs so that you can produce a clear job description. Be specific and realistic. Nannies cannot do all your housework, laundry, and errands and still provide quality care for three children.

2. **Initial phone interview**: Spread the word. Tell everybody you know that you are looking for a nanny. Some of the best nannies never look for work in ads but are passed on from family to family. You can first call an agency and learn what you must know. If you do put an advertisement on line or in the newspaper, you may get a large response. Have some key questions ready by the phone that you can use to screen applicants (schedule, experience, driving requirements, recent references, etc).

3. **Interview:** Have the candidate come to your home for an interview when your children are home. Watch how she plays or talks to them. The interview is a give-and-take exercise. Tell the candidate about your children's interests, the start date and length of commitment, the weekly schedules and likely variations to expect. Explain any additional household duties, salary, travel required with your family, and benefits (paid vacation, sick time, health insurance). Try not to overwhelm or intimidate the candidate. She may be shy with adults but shine with children.

   Here are some sample questions to ask the candidate:

- What do you enjoy most and least about working with kids?
- Describe a day with my children. What will you do on a rainy day?
- How do you handle stubborn behavior? Refusal to nap? A temper tantrum?
- How do you deal with the isolation of a nanny job?
- Under what circumstances do you think it appropriate to call me at work?
- Will all your references remember you? Did all these jobs end happily?

Trust you instincts. If a candidate makes you uneasy on the phone or when you meet her, thank her for calling or coming, but don't spend any more time checking references. You need to have complete trust in this important new member of your household.

4. **Check references:** This is the most important part of the process. Be certain to ask about reliability, responsibility, flexibility, limit-setting techniques, and how the children felt about the applicant. If she is going to drive carpools for you, you may want to check her driving record. Some parents also do a background check (including criminal record, credit report, and social security verification).
5. **Have a trial period:** If everything you have felt and discovered about this candidate is good, you may want to invite her back for an evening or day to baby-sit. At the end of this trial, be prepared to offer her the job. Good nannies often have many job options open to them, and they may read a prolonged process as disinterest.

Keys to a successful nanny-family relationship

Put everything in writing. Take the job description and make it into a work agreement that you both sign. This work agreement should include the nanny's duties, hours, the handling of taxes, benefits, telephone calls, private times, and the plan for ongoing communication and review of these agreements.

Communicate on a weekly basis. Create a special time to check in with one another each week to discuss the children, the schedule, or anything else that comes to mind—without pressure. Most nanny-family problems are small things that go unspoken, and then turn into big problems. An example would be if the nanny were to return home late from time off, request that she calls you so that you don't worry about where she is or what may have happened to her.

Treat the nanny with respect. This is her place of employment, and you are her supervisor.

Meet your time obligations. It is so tempting to stop off at the store or do an errand, knowing the kids are in the hands of their nanny. But repeated lateness will affect your nanny in the same way that her lateness would affect you.

Appreciate your nanny. A small gift or bonus after a particularly difficult week can make a huge difference in a long-term relationship. Nannies that feel unappreciated often look for work elsewhere, and these transitions can be very difficult for your children.

Feng Shui: The Route to Harmony

Feng Shui is the ancient Chinese art of placement based on respect for the order, harmony, and balance of nature. I have shown you how to combine some knowledge of the forces of the universe with a practical approach to environmental planning. By enhancing the flow of chi energy and balancing yin and yang, you will simplify your life, gain a clearer mind and healthier body, and find the energy to be a better parent and have fun with your family and friends. Ultimately, you will create happiness for all the members of your family.

Feng Shui is not just one more thing to add to an already hectic life with little time to stop and think. If you spend your time dashing between work and home and cramming your appointment calendar with things to do, you need Feng Shui. It will help you evaluate the dissatisfaction you feel with your daily environment and routine, transforming them into a more fulfilled life for all members of the family. Feng Shui is your route to a more harmonious existence.

A misplaced chair, desk, or table, or an ill-conceived color scheme can produce a chain reaction that leads to disharmony in other parts of your life. Feng Shui is more complex than interior design—it is a highly personal venture and way of living. Many people have been convinced of its value once they have implemented its principles and experienced its value.

I am also a parent, and I am always looking for ways to provide children with balance in their lives, self-esteem, learning, and love. This book is an expression of my commitment to the children of the world.

If you have unsolved questions, feel free to e-mail me at nstohn324@hotmail.com. My intention is for you to use Feng Shui in your lives on a continual basis.

My Workbook:

This workbook section will focus on areas for you to take immediate action. I want you to make the necessary changes to affect the incoming chi energy, which will in turn affect the moods of your family members, the flow of communication of ideas, as well as their overall health. Use the Bagua drawings provided to map each area of your home.

The Exterior

- Stand at your front door and look outwards. Are there any large structures or objects pointing at your front door, generating what Feng Shui refers to as "secret arrows"? It might be telephone poles and wires, a telecommunications satellite, or a long straight road aimed at your property. To counter this bad chi energy, place an eight-sided Bagua mirror over your front door. This mirror will protect the house from oncoming traffic.
- The access to your front door should be flat, or sloping slightly, so that chi energy can flow smoothly towards your home. If the path leading to your front door slopes away from the house, a row of shrubs or small trees will help to slow the chi energy running away from the site.
- When the front path or driveway is evenly curved, the chi energy flows gently towards the house. The driveway for a car should curve around towards the side of the house and the footpath should lead from the driveway to your front door.
- There should only be one pathway to your front door so there is no confusion.
- There should be no rubbish or recycling bins around your front door.
- Plant bushes or trees of unequal sizes and shape on each side of your front door.

The Front Door

Your front door is the pathway for chi energy to enter your home. If the entrance is narrow, hang a brass wind chime over whichever door you regularly use to enter your home. The door must be clean, freshly painted, and in good working condition. There should not be piles of newspapers or magazines, or shoes dropped randomly inside the doorway. Install adequate lighting so your entrance is clearly visible. Ensure that your doorbell or doorknocker functions properly.

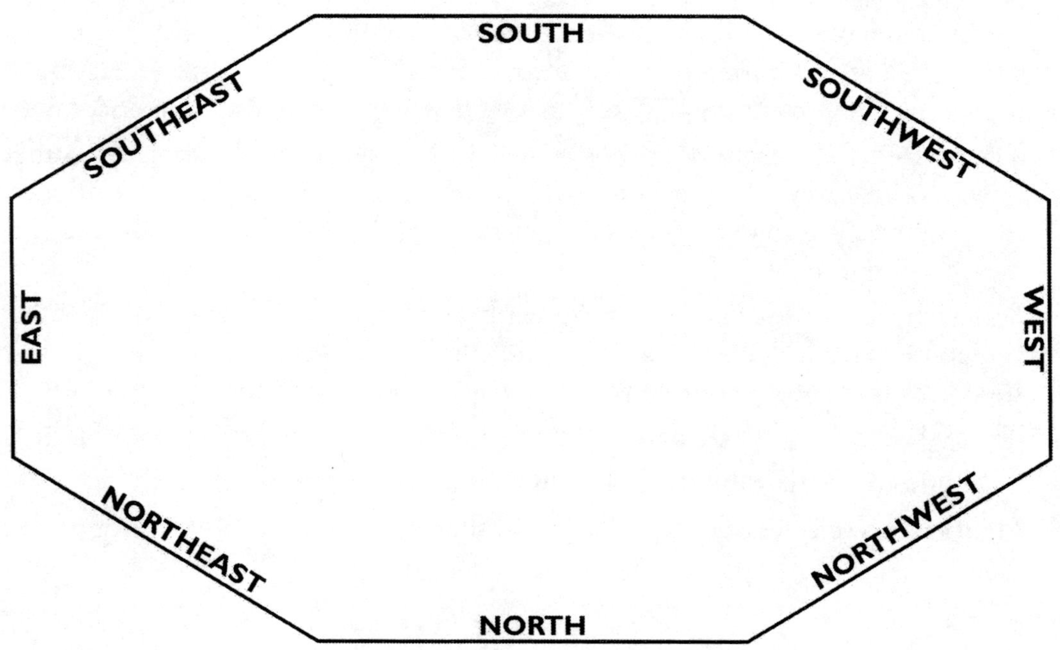

The Foyer or Entrance Hall

Your foyer or entrance hall should contain a table or chest of drawers. This provides a convenient place for people entering and leaving your home to place their keys, eyeglasses, or briefcases and handbags. You might choose to place flowers or a plant on it as well. Neatly organize your front hall closet with enough extra hangers and space for guests.

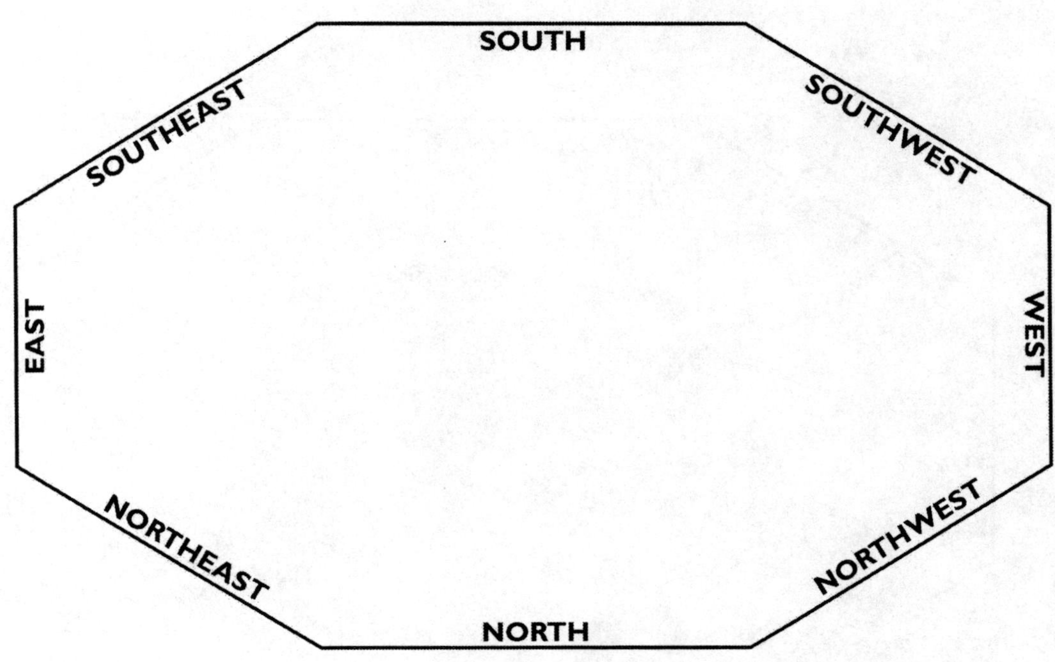

The Living Room

Your living room or gathering room exists for your family to entertain guests and to come together to socialize. Arrange seating into "conversation groups" that enable everyone to communicate easily with each other. Keep tops of tables clean and plants healthy. Keep CDs and DVDs in their designated place. Keep passageways through this room clear to allow easy access. Provide a variety of lighting sources with low and high levels for reading, playing games, and socializing.

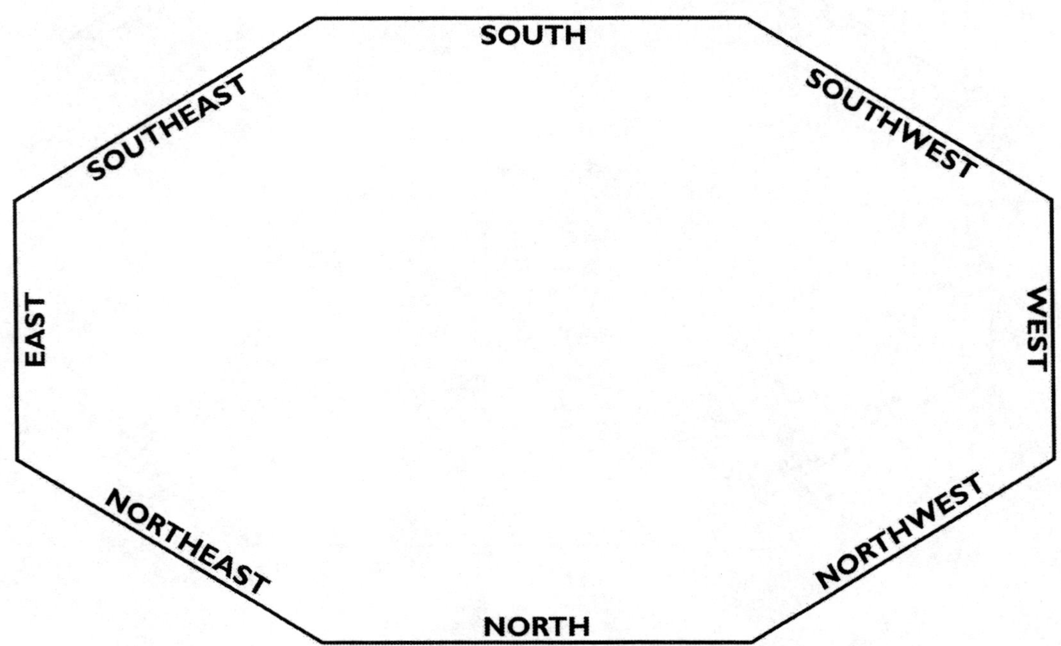

The Kitchen

Your kitchen represents abundance and wealth and provides your family with nourishment. You can place a mirror in the back of your stove's burners, which will double the chi energy and your abundance. Use your stove regularly, even if it's only to boil water. Keep passageways clear. Keep the kitchen counters clear and clean, cabinets neat, and appliances in good working condition. Discard expired food products from your pantry, refrigerator, and freezer. Try not to eat on the run. Try not to have arguments during meals, which can upset your digestion.

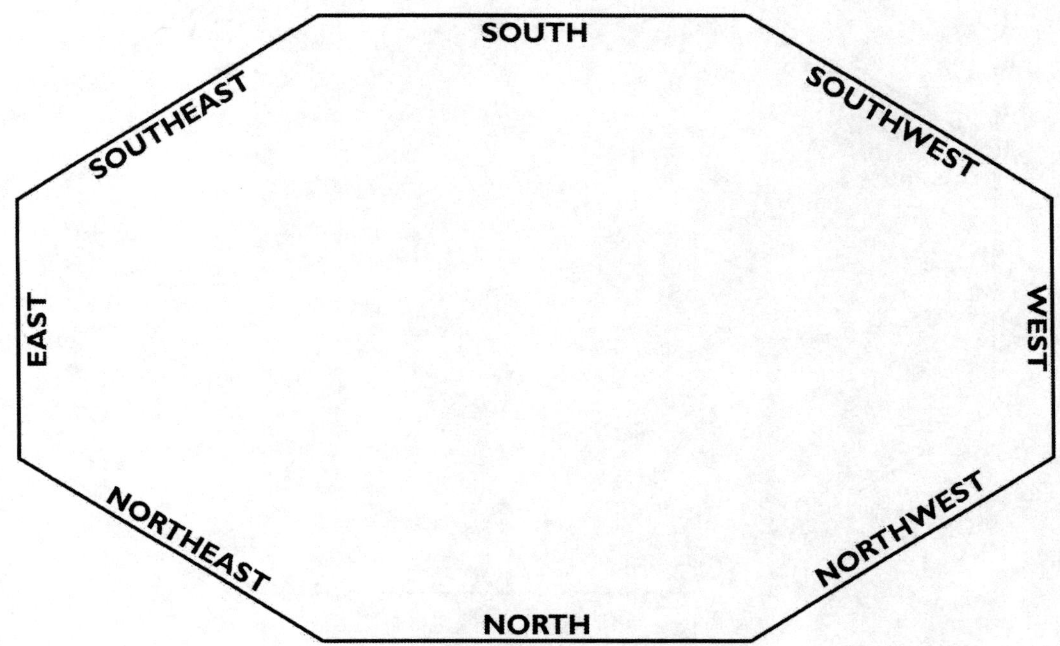

The Dining Room

Your dining room affects your health because it is the place where you are nourished and interact socially with your family and guests. Establish a peaceful, congenial environment. Repair or replace any broken furniture as it can indicate breaks in personal or business relationships. And again, clear any clutter that might have previously been a project and is still lingering on the dining room table.

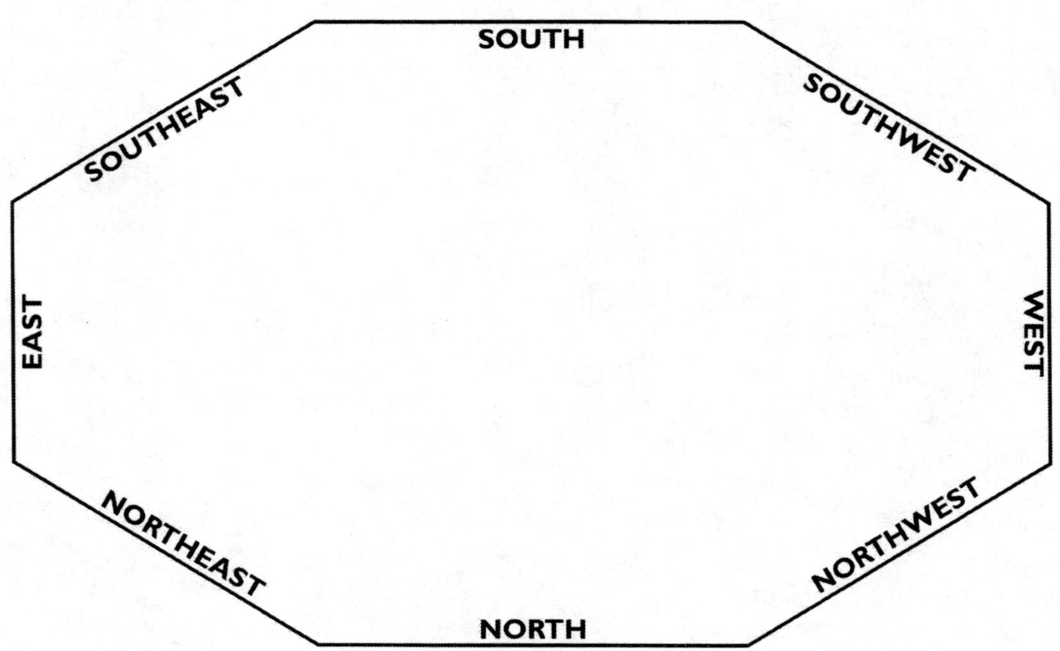

The Master Bedroom

Don't put your headboard and bed on the bathroom wall or in front of a window. Clear out whatever is stored under your bed. Check what is on your night table and clear out the clutter. Watch how the relationship with your partner becomes more relaxed in time after you have made these changes.

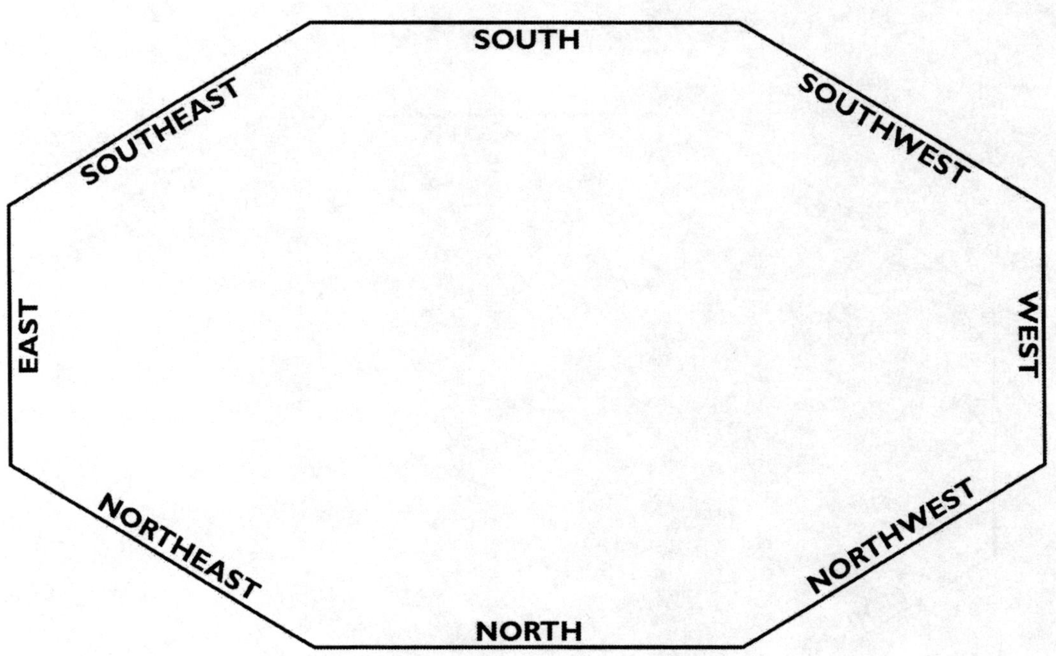

The Bathroom

Bathrooms are areas of elimination, where wastes are flushed away. The chi energy is flushed out of your house via the toilet and bathroom drains. Fix dripping faucets or toilets that run and waste water. The Chinese believe that open drains and open toilet lids tend to suck the chi energy, and ultimately the wealth, out of your home. Keep your bathrooms clean, as germs collect and multiply in a dirty bathroom. Use bright lights to balance the yin and yang in these rooms.

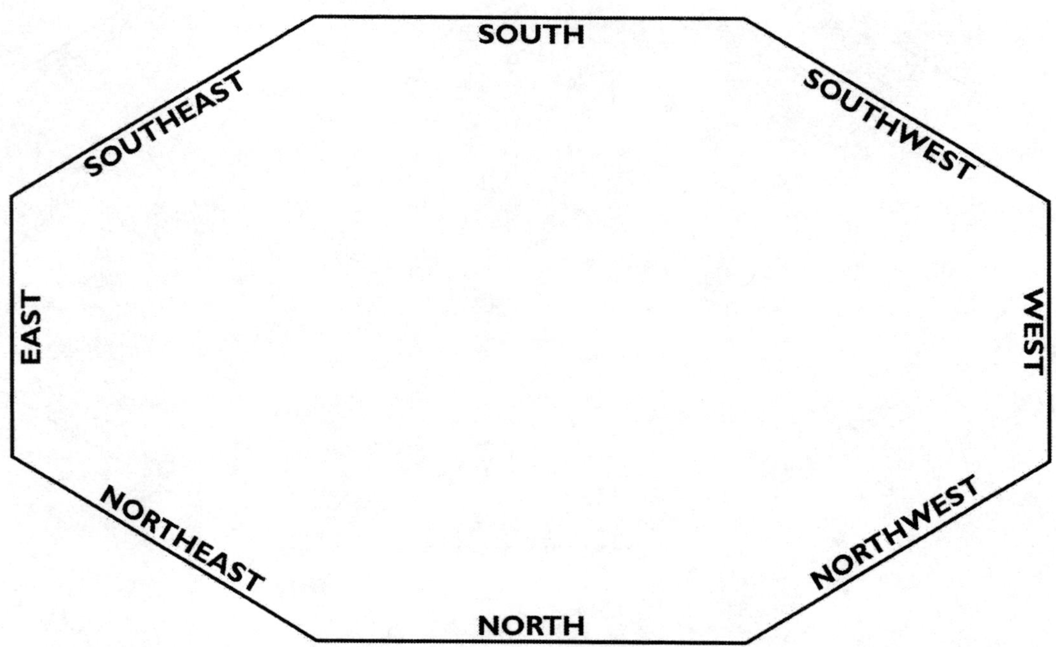

The Teenager's Room

The teenager's room should reflect the occupant. It might have images posted on the wall that reflect good times, motivational pictures that are personal, or positive phrases or words. Nothing should be stored under the bed and no laundry should be gathering in a corner or on the floor to block the chi energy. Make sure the bed is easy to be "made," as well as comfortable for sleep, with a good pillow and a bedside lamp with a clock. Assist your teenagers in creating their personalized "sanctuaries."

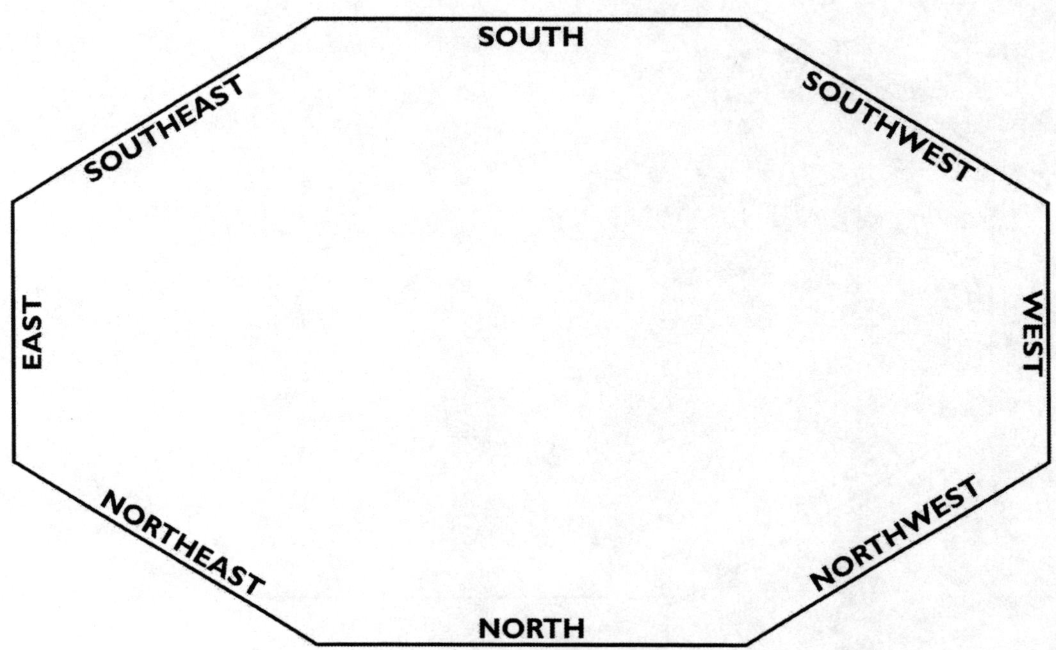

The Child's Room

Children's rooms should contain a comfortable bed, with enough room for the child to sleep in, along with their stuffed animals. Place a lamp for reading books on the night table. Provide easy access to clothing for children to choose clothes to dress themselves, as well as to store clothes. Do not store anything under the bed and do not hang anything over the headboard. These measures will ensure a good night's sleep for the children, allowing their souls to relax.

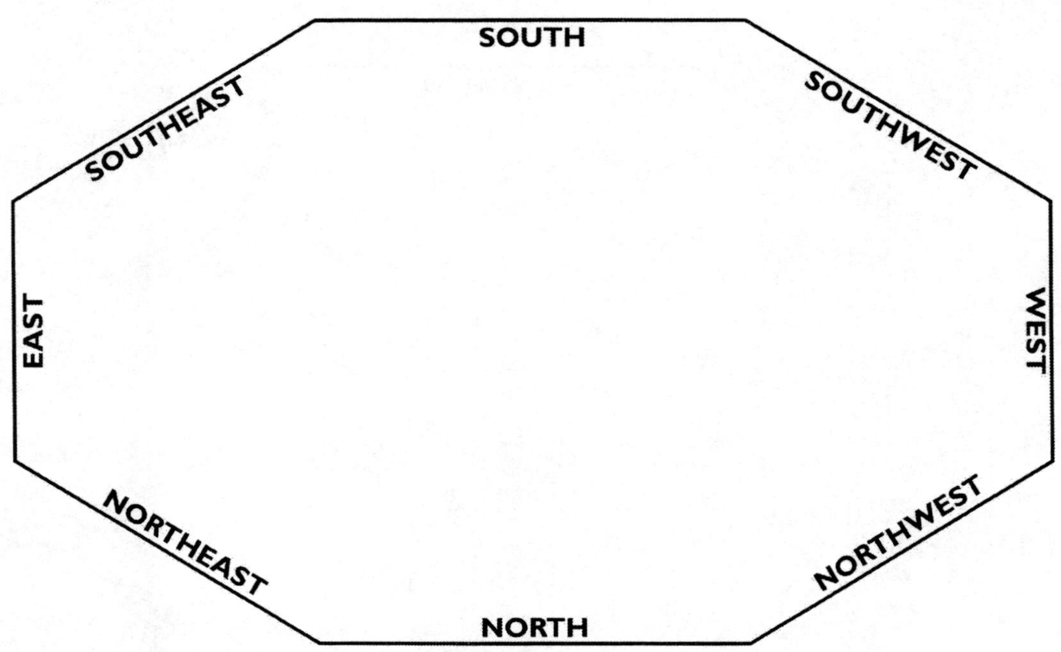

My Accomplishments Are:

- ❐ I have used the Bagua to map out my master bedroom.

____

____

- ❐ I have determined the Feng Shui cures to use and put them in place.

____

____

- ❐ I have removed all clutter.

____

____

- ❐ I have achieved a sense of freedom.

____

____

- ❐ I FEEL BETTER!

____

____

- ❐ I now want to let the chi flow smoothly throughout the rest of my HOME and LIFE.

____

____

Continuing on...

BIBLIOGRAPHY

Beattie, Antonia, and Rosemary Stevens, *Unclutter Your Space with Feng Shui*, Barnes & Noble Books, New York, 2001.

Brown, Simon, *Feng Shui for Business*, Ward Lock, London, 1998.

———, *Feng Shui Solutions*, Cassell & Co., London, 2000.

Englebert, Clear, *Feng Shui Demystified*, Crossing Press, Santa Cruz, CA., 2000.

Gallagher, Winifred, *The Power of Place*, Harper Collins Publishers, Inc., New York, 1993.

Hale, Gill, *The Practical Encyclopedia of Feng Shui*, Anness Publishing Limited, London, 2001

Jenkins, Peggy, *The Joyful Child*, Harbinger House, Inc., Tucson, AZ, 1989.

Lagatree, Kristen M., *Feng Shui*, Villard Books, New York, 1996.

Kwok, Man-Ho, *Chinese Astrology*, Tuttle Publishing, Boston, 1997.

Marks, David Ryan, *Raising Stable Kids In An Unstable World*, Health Communications, Inc., Deerfield Beach, FL, 2002.

Rossbach, Sarah, *Feng Shui: The Chinese Art of Placement*, Penguin Books USA, Inc., New York, 1983.

Sharp Damian, *Simple Feng Shui*, Conari Press, Berkeley, CA, 1999.

Thompson, Angel, *Feng Shui: How to Achieve the Most Harmonious Arrangements of Your Home and Office*, St. Martin's Griffin, New York, 1996.

Too, Lillian, *Creating Abundance with Feng Shui*, Ballantine Wellspring Books, New York, 1999.

Wydra, Nancilee, *Feng Shui for Children's Spaces*, Contemporary Books, Lincolnwood (Chicago), IL, 2001.

Xing, Wu, *The Feng Shui Work Book*, Tuttle Publishing, Boston, 1998.

ISBN 1-41204342-5

9 781412 043427